The Somali Cat

Dianne Taylor

Bright Pen

Visit us online at www.authorsonline.co.uk

A Bright Pen Book

Copyright © Dianne Taylor 2014

Cover design by Emma Watts ©

British Library Cataloguing Publication Data.
A catalogue record for this book is available from the British Library

ISBN 978-0-7552-1619-2

Authors OnLine Ltd
19 The Cinques
Gamlingay, Sandy
Bedfordshire SG19 3NU
England

www.authorsonline.co.uk

About the Author

I began breeding cats in 1980. My original breed was Burmese, but in 1986 I acquired my first Somali and my love affair with these charming cats began; it continues to this day. I have run a boarding cattery for over thirty years and am proud that it is FAB approved. I have served on many cat club committees, including The Somali Cat Club. This book is designed to give information about the Somali breed, with advice on breeding, showing and general care of the cat and the opinions expressed herein are solely those of the author and are based entirely upon my experience of living, working with and owning cats for over forty years.

This book is dedicated to the memory of my beloved Cracker, who represents all the Somalis who have been owned and loved by their human slaves and also to the memory of Jo and Colin Hubert, who by their generous bequest, secured the future of those Somalis who are in need of Somali Cat Club Welfare.

All author royalties from the sale of this book go to

Somali Cat Club Welfare

CONTENTS

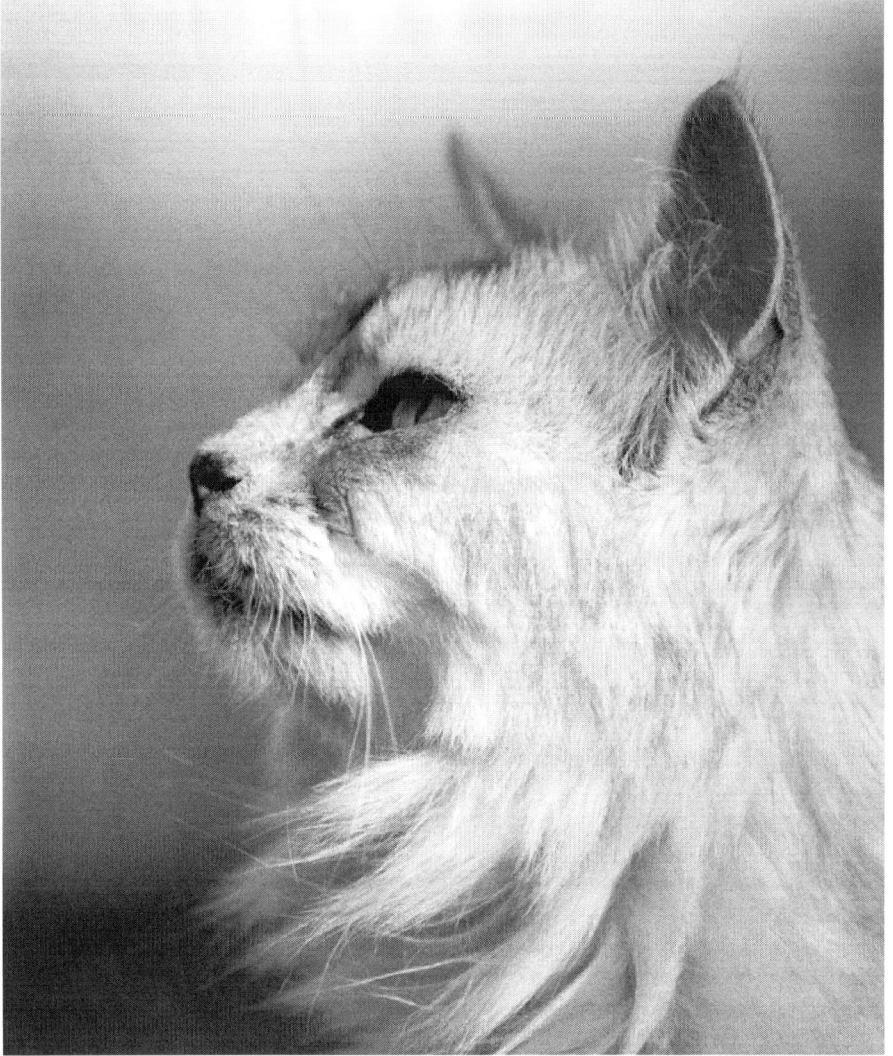

Chapter 1. The History of the Somali Breed

The Somali breed owes its origins to the Abyssinian breed. From time to time kittens would be produced from supposedly pure Abyssinian cats with an atypical colour or hair type. An occasional 'oddity' can be dismissed as a chance mutation, but when that 'oddity' appears in litters with shared ancestors, it is far more likely that a recessive gene is present which will never disappear but be passed on to at least some of the offspring. This is exactly what happened with the Abyssinian and Somali breeds.

The Somali story really begins in America in 1967 when two Abyssinian parents gave birth to a long hair kitten which was named George. His mother was Lo-Mi-R's Trill-by and his father was Lynn-Lees Lord Dublin. The owner of Trill-by was far from enthusiastic about this fluffy and poor example of an Abyssinian so, at only five weeks old, she gave him away and told Evelyn Mague (the owner of his father) that he had disappeared. A short while later Evelyn acquired Trill-by when her owner gave up breeding and then, by an extraordinary twist of fate, she became the owner of George. Evelyn worked at a cat rescue centre and when a Longhaired Abyssinian was brought in to be re-homed, she realised from his paperwork that it was George. Sadly, because of his temperament, he was unable to be bred from so he was neutered and re-homed. However, Evelyn realised that as she now owned both of his parents, she had the means to breed more like him, so with great care, she did several repeat matings and produced more long haired kittens.

After a great deal of thought, Evelyn decided upon SOMALI as a name for these beautiful long hair Abyssinians. Their roots are in the Abyssinian breed, and as Somalia borders onto Ethiopia (originally called Abyssinia), people will always remember the origins of the Somali breed. In the early days the new breed was not welcomed by the Aby breeders; many refused to admit their cats might carry the long hair gene, while some said the pedigrees were fake and that Persians had been deliberately crossed with Abyssinians.

Somalis were ostracised at shows with some breeders even being told to neuter their cats and not attend shows with them. Understandably, Evelyn was discouraged by the attitude of the established Abyssinian breeders but persevered – eventually, after placing an advert in a cat magazine for over twelve months appealing for an Aby breeder to sell her a longhair kitten, she received a reply from Don Richings of the Don Al cattery in Canada. His cats, Dunedin Moseph and Don Al's Marsue, produced two longhair kittens which were able to found another Somali breeding line. At last, the Somali breed could progress.

In 1972, Evelyn founded the Somali Cat Club of America and by then the Somalis were attracting admirers; they were doing favourably at shows and this success encouraged some Abyssinian breeders to admit they had longhaired kittens. The first longhaired kittens to be openly registered from supposedly pure Abyssinian parents were Mei-Lens Topaze, Toujours Ragamuffin, Golden Boise, and Du-Ro-Al's Samson. Patricia Nell Warren joined the Somali campaign and her tireless work meant the breed was recognised by the CFA in 1977. It had taken ten long years to achieve this recognition.

In 1980 the Somali came to the UK. A consortium of breeders imported two Somalis from the USA, Foxtails Belle Star and Ch. Nephranis Omar Khayyam. Shortly afterwards Black Iron Vagabond and Black Iron Venus were imported. Over the next four or five years, many more Somalis were imported from both the US and Australia; these dedicated breeders spent a great deal of time and money enabling the breed to become established quickly in the UK. The early breeders included Patricia Brownsell, Alistair and Phyl Cassels, Margaret and Peter Frayne, June Good, Anne Rose and Ann Watson.

All the early breeders realised just how closely related the imported cats were and so, to ensure the gene pool could be widened, they sought the approval of the GCCF to outcross with Abyssinians. This was agreed as it was vital for maintaining the health and vigour of the breed. In 1981, the Somali Cat Club was formed with over seventy members. The Club set strict rules to prevent known variants (shorthair cats known to carry the longhair gene) being used to breed Abyssinians so that the longhair gene could not be introduced into what should be a pure short hair breed. This rule is still strictly adhered to.

I am glad to say that as the years have rolled by, the Somali has steadily increased in popularity and they and their owners are welcomed by the Abyssinian breeders and Clubs. Often the Somali is affectionately referred to as The Abyssinian in an overcoat.

Chapter 2. The Personality of the Somali

To truly appreciate the personality of the Somali we need to understand what a cat really is. The ancestors of today's cats evolved about 45 million years ago and they looked and behaved much like the cats of today. There are three main groups of cats: the PANTHER, which consists of lions and tigers and other big cats, the CHEETAH, which has a group all of its own called ACINONYX because of the inability to retract the claws and the third group, FELIS, which includes pumas, lynxes and other small wildcats along with their most famous descendent, FELIS CATUS CATUS, the domesticated cat that we share our homes with.

The first cats were domesticated between five and eight thousand years ago in the Nile Valley in Egypt. As man learned to farm and became less nomadic, members of the African wildcat family were drawn to domesticity. Farmers stored grain which attracted rats and in turn attracted the wild cat because of the supply of food. The farmers encouraged the cats to stay and continue the job of protecting the crops: liking a steady supply of food and the freedom from danger, the cats were happy to remain. These early domesticated cats were different from the African wild cat as they enjoyed human contact; researchers believe that there was a genetic mutation which made some of the African wild cats more adaptable to human companionship. Over the years, through natural selection, these more gentle mutant cats became the ancestors of our fireside cats of today.

In history the cat has experienced chequered fortunes. In ancient Egypt the cat was worshipped and was so honoured that the penalty for killing a cat was death. When a cat died the entire household went into mourning and as a mark of respect, wailed and lamented and shaved their eyebrows. The cat would be embalmed and wrapped in a linen sheet; the mummified cat would be placed in a coffin and was often accompanied by mummified rats and shrews as food in the afterlife. The mummified bodies were taken to burial sites: there was one such site in Beni Hasan where in the late nineteenth century hundreds of thousands of mummified cats were unearthed.

Cats had been domesticated in Egypt for at least a thousand years before they began to spread to other countries and they did not reach Europe until well after the birth of Christ. Through interbreeding with the European wildcat, the appearance of the cat began to alter and become stockier and broader than the lean, elegant felines of Egypt. That difference is still apparent today: compare the elegant foreign-type body of the Somali with that of the British Shorthair breed. The first cats in Britain were revered for their mousing abilities and anyone who killed a cat would be severely penalised by having to give up a lamb or a sheep. However, in Europe, in the Middle Ages, the reverence for the cat was replaced by fear and loathing. The cat was seen to be associated with witchcraft and thus began a long period of abuse and cruelty. Historians believe that the drastic diminution of the cat population caused by this persecution contributed to the spread of bubonic plague, a disease caused by a bacterium living on the fleas which lived on rats. With fewer mousers, the rats ran riot. As people suffered, they did not have time to persecute cats so their numbers increased and inevitably, those of the rat reduced. By the eighteenth century, the hostility towards cats was waning and slowly they became valued pets once more.

The basic body structure and appearance of the cat has changed very little through history although people did not begin to notice or value the different breeds of cat until Victorian times. The variety of breeds gives choice of colour, fur length, and temperament. Owning a pedigree cat enables a person to find the temperament and personality that best suits their needs and lifestyle.

In my job I meet all breeds of cats but for me the personality of the Somali makes it stand out. I am proud to admit I am biased as I share my home and life with these wonderful creatures. I doubt very much that whatever I write can do justice to the personality of the Somali as is almost impossible to be objective when you are in love! The Somali is a medium sized cat and everything about the physique is moderate: there are no exaggerations in the head or body. The Somali does have a unique feature: the set of the jaw is such that it makes the cat appear to smile and a true Somali always has a smiling expression and this particular characteristic is included in the standard of points for the breed. Perhaps because they are smiling cats, they are happy little souls with a great sense of fun.

Somalis are 'people' cats and you will never be alone when you share your life with them: I always say that owning the Somali is the nearest you will get in the cat world to owning a dog. They adore their people and will follow you where ever you go. They are easy to train to a harness and no job in the home can be completed without supervision and 'help' from a Somali. Even personal activities are interrupted by their presence: on many occasions, whilst having a bath, a Somali has sat on the side watching intently and sometimes they have even slipped into the bath. This does not faze them at all as they have a fascination with water. One of my queens played in her water bowl so enthusiastically that I had to invest in a special bowl which she could not overturn.

Somalis are mischievous cats who are always ready to play and even as they get older, they remain youthful in their outlook on life and continue to be energetic. They are extroverts and enjoy attention: for this reason I would not advise anyone who is away from home all day and has no other pets to have a Somali, as they need and seek companionship. Somalis will interact with other animals: my own Somalis live happily with my dogs, although the dogs know that the cats are boss! On winter nights, my cats like to lie by the fire and so do my very large dogs, causing the heat to be blocked from the cats. My Somalis have managed to overcome this problem very easily, having discovered that the one thing my dogs hate is having their ears washed. With a very attentive Somali on ear cleaning duty, the dog has no option but to move away and the empty space is filled immediately by the cats; who says dogs are more intelligent than cats! They interact well with most breeds of cats but care should be taken when mixing them with Turkish Vans or Bengals as the gentle nature of the

The Somali Cat

Somali can encourage breeds with more dominant personalities to bully them. Somalis are the perfect family pet as they relate well to children: my own children grew up with them and they never used tooth or claw and now with my grandchildren history is repeating itself.

I find it very sad that some cats are re-homed when a baby arrives on the scene: with common sense, the baby and the cat can live in perfect harmony. I am a firm believer that children benefit from living with pets, learning compassion and how to care for a vulnerable creature. These are lessons they will continue to employ throughout their lives. When I brought my own twins home from hospital and introduced them to the cats, they were naturally curious about these pink miniature humans but accepted them readily. When my children were six, I offered them the chance to own a kitten themselves and left the choice to them. Vicky was slow to choose her kitten but eventually she met her soul mate and here begins the story of an extraordinary relationship between feline and child.

I had a litter of three kittens and as they grew it was clear one of the kittens was not faring as well as his siblings. I kept a careful eye on him and suddenly he developed jaundice. A trip to the vet confirmed my worst fears; his liver was not functioning properly and the prognosis was poor. On my return home, Vicky asked what the vet had said and on hearing the dismal news, she announced this was the kitten she wanted to keep. I tried to dissuade her, knowing it would bring heartache, but she had set her mind to raising this kitten. Raffles, as we called him, then moved into Vicky's bedroom; they slept together, they ate together, she would carry him everywhere and he became addicted to children's TV. Slowly he recovered and the liver (an organ which can regenerate) repaired itself. By now, cat and child were inseparable and Raffles would wait by the door for his young mistress to return from school. There were many ups and downs whilst Raffles was recovering but Vicky stood by him through thick and thin. He turned into a beautiful cat and won many classes at shows but to Vicky, win or lose, he was the best cat ever. My daughter was a young woman when Raffles suffered a stroke and sadly this time Vicky could not save him; it was a very miserable mum and daughter who drove back from the vet with Raffles for burial in the garden. We decided to bury him under Vicky's bedroom window where he had spent so much of his life. Vicky has cats of her own to this day, but she will be the first to admit they don't quite match Raffles.

Cats which live in harmony with each other will spend a great deal of time in mutual grooming; be prepared, the Somali will also groom its owner. They love to sit perched on your shoulder, rubbing against your face; this will progress to cleaning your face very gently, although the rough tongue of a cat can be quite abrasive. This is only the beginning; having cleaned the face, the Somali will turn its attentions to restyling your hair - my cats will groom my hair into styles that Vidal Sassoon never dreamt of. I had a dear neuter whose passion in life was to rearrange everyone's hair - much to his bemusement, we were visited one day by a completely bald gentleman. Blue had never encountered this before and began licking the bald pate; logically, he thought the hair must be somewhere and proceeded to dig his claws into the head looking for it! Our visitor made a hasty retreat - I can't imagine why! As far as a Somali is concerned, their owner's nose is there to be licked and ears are to be affectionately nibbled. To a Somali, the best place in the world is draped around their owner's neck like a living fur collar with paws kneading the air in ecstasy. Somalis have a firm belief that laps are there for sitting on and will curl up contentedly and sleep.

Somalis are busy cats - they rush everywhere, investigating all in their path. The breed has been likened to a fox because of their bushy tail which they hold high in the air when they are happy, rather like a banner flying in the wind. I can think of no better sight than being greeted by a Somali with tail held high and fluffy breeches wiggling in a seductive manner, better than any model on a cat walk could imitate. To add to this, they will talk to you and because of the unique set of the jaw they do not miaow but chirrup like a bird.

The Somali Cat

The Somali is an intelligent cat; they always manage to get their owners to do exactly as they want! Some cats will rush up a tree and then get stuck; not the Somali. It will sit at the bottom, weigh up the logistics and decide not to over reach itself. They will retrieve toys and even open doors, particularly the fridge! You will never be bored living with a Somali. If given freedom to roam, they are terrific hunters. Some years ago I sold a kitten to a farmer; his workers were horrified that he had bought a pedigree cat (or as they said a posh cat) - what use would that be? It did not take the workforce long to discover that Mac was probably the best hunter they had ever had. He spent his days keeping the mice at bay and one of his favourite pastimes was to hitch a ride with his master on the tractor. In the evenings he whiled away his time by the fire in the farmhouse. When Mac passed away (an elderly gentleman by then) it was the workforce who insisted the farmer 'go and get one of those posh cats'!

If I had to sum up the personality of the Somali it would be Stunning Outgoing Mischievous Affectionate Loyal Inquisitive.

Chapter 3. Choosing a Kitten

When choosing a kitten there are a number of questions you should ask yourself. Firstly, you need to decide on a breed and I am assuming that as you are reading this book, your interest lies in Somalis. Different breeds have different personality traits so make sure you choose a breed that will fit into your lifestyle and meet your requirements. Visit cat shows and meet breeders and their cats, but best of all go to breeder's homes to see the cats in their own environment. Remember, you are about to embark on a commitment that could last for eighteen years or more. The next question you should ask yourself is; why do you want a kitten? Is it to be purely a pet or do you wish to show or breed in the future? Whatever the reason, you are looking for a new member of the home who will need love and care for the rest their life. Remember: dogs have masters but cats have slaves!

The Somali Cat Club has a web site where breeders can advertise their kittens for sale. Any breeder using this site must have signed a declaration agreeing to abide by the Club's guidelines, which are set to ensure that kittens are reared responsibly. The GCCF also has a Breeder Scheme which promotes responsible breeding and breeders are monitored to make sure they follow the code of ethics set out in the scheme.

When you are buying a kitten, for whatever reason, there are certain key factors to bear in mind. When you visit the kittens, the breeder should let you meet the mum. An outgoing, confident mother will be happy to let visitors handle her kittens and she will have taught those characteristics to her offspring. If the owner of the queen also owns the sire, you may even be able to meet him. Do not be surprised if, when you first arrive, the kittens are reticent; they will be naturally suspicious of unfamiliar people, but once strangers sit down and begin to play with them, their innate curiosity will bring them to the fore. It is important to observe how the kittens have been reared; personally, if I was shown a kitten kept in a pen, I would walk away there and then, because it would not be socialised and this can present major problems with temperament later in life. All kittens should be reared in the house and familiar with household noises and furnishings. Having said that, very few of my kittens like the vacuum cleaner and scurry away from it, but they do like my bed!

It is also important to observe the environment the kittens are living in; there should be plenty of litter trays (ideally one per kitten) and it should be evident that these are cleaned on a regular basis; food in bowls should also be fresh. The environment should smell fresh and clean and the kitten's coats should be free from debris and parasites such as fleas. Should the breeder rearing the kittens not employ good husbandry, this will have an effect on their health. Over the years I have given advice to people who have bought kittens from back street breeders and they have paid the price in vet bills and heartache. I always query why they bought the kitten and in every case the answer is the same; they felt sorry for it and wanted to rescue it from the situation. Although this is an understandable reaction, it is short sighted because it perpetuates the problem and more kittens will be born into the same environment. However hard it is, my advice would be to walk away and seek a kitten from a conscientious breeder.

You must also decide what colour kitten you want and what sex. There are 28 different colours of Somalis to choose from. The original colour was Usual which is a rich golden brown ticked with black. This gives the Somali a slightly 'wild' or natural look. Sorrel is a rich apricot colour. Blue Somalis can be of any shade of blue but the undercoat should be a warm mushroom. The Fawn is a warm powdery colour. There are also Chocolates, Lilacs, Reds and Creams. All these colours also come in the silver version; a Usual Silver Somali is silvery white with black ticking and resembles the Arctic fox. The Sorrel Silver is silvery white with cinnamon ticking, conjuring up the image of peaches and cream. There are also many Tortie and Tortie Silver colours which help to make up the 28 colours on offer. Whatever the colour, there are two things that all Somalis have, the first of which is ticking. Each hair of a Somali will have bands of colour all along its length, at least 6 and possibly as many as 14. The bands are made up of alternate lines of base coat colour (e.g. apricot in the Sorrel) and ticking colour (e.g. cinnamon in the Sorrel). Ticking is one of the things that help to give the Somali its unique look and it is the essence of the Somali. The other attribute all Somalis share is their wonderful loving nature, regardless of what colour they are.

Over the years I have met many people who have visited to choose a kitten; they know which sex they want and which colour but almost inevitably leave my home having booked something completely different because the personality of a particular kitten has appealed to them. A litter of kittens will all have been reared in the same way and encountered the same environment but they are all individuals and display different personalities; choose the one that best suits you. No kitten from a registered breeder will be allowed to leave until it is at least 13 weeks old, by which time a full course of vaccinations will have been completed. The kittens will be registered with a governing body and you will be given a copy of their pedigree. Most kittens are also insured for the first 4 weeks in their new home. The breeder should also give you a detailed diet sheet so there is as little change as possible in your kitten's diet.

Some people want a pedigree kitten so they can take up the hobby of showing their cat. I have shown cats for over thirty years and have made many good friends over that time and it is a hobby I would be happy to recommend to anyone. There are shows held throughout the country nearly every Saturday so you will have plenty of opportunity to show your cat. I would advise that if you are new to the breed, you take the advice of the breeder as to which kittens in the litter have show potential. No breeder who is proud of their cats would wish to see a pet quality kitten shown as it reflects on the standard of their prefix so be guided by them. There is one maxim I have used throughout my showing career; love the cat, not the win - you will always take the best cat to the show and you will always bring the best cat home with you.

Some people are keen to breed cats themselves, but before you embark on this hobby there are a number of questions you must ask yourself. Once you begin breeding, the cat population in the home will inevitably expand, so according to the space available, you must decide upon the maximum number of cats you can accommodate with their wellbeing paramount. There may be times when you are unable to sell all of the kittens in a litter; should this arise, you will need to have a contingency plan. What are you going to do when a queen is retired? Will you keep her or re-home her? Personally, I do not re-home my girls as I feel they have given me so much and have earned their retirement in the environment they know, but I am fortunate in that I have plenty of space in the house.

If you decide to go ahead, you are about to embark upon a hobby that will be a roller coaster of emotions. It is very rewarding and there is no better sight than a queen safely delivered of her litter and the kittens all on the milk bar! However, you must be prepared for heartache as not all the kittens will survive and the longer you breed the more likely you are to encounter problems which, statistically, you cannot avoid forever. For a novice breeder, the best help you can get is from another breeder happy to act as your mentor. Join the Somali Cat Club as the Club has a network of people all ready and willing to offer advice and help. Established breeders are always pleased to encourage enthusiastic, responsible newcomers as it secures the future of the breed. When you are buying a kitten for breeding, be guided by the breeder as to the suitability of the kitten. I do have very definite views on this subject; some breeders will sell a kitten for breeding but state that it is not show quality. It is of paramount importance that you only breed from the very best examples and if a cat is not good enough to be shown, it is certainly not good enough for breeding. The whole aim of breeding should be to produce better and better examples of the breed. In her breeding life, a queen may give birth to around twenty kittens. During his breeding life, a stud cat is capable of siring hundreds of kittens and thus an inferior stud can do untold damage to the standard of the breed for many years to come. I do not advise anyone to own a stud until they have had several years of breeding experience and enough queens to keep the stud contented. Stud work is very rewarding, but also time consuming and carries with it great responsibility. The stud owner needs to have enough knowledge to support the owner of a visiting queen if they seek advice.

I have bred cats for over thirty years and have learnt in that time that it can be difficult and time consuming; breeding good examples of the breed with health, type and temperament takes dedication, courage, love and the strength to withstand heartache. The resources required are space, time, sound finances, and a team of supportive people. Personally, I cannot imagine life without kittens running around the house and over the years I have spent thousands of pounds with my vet. If I had not bred cats, financially I might well be a wealthy woman by now, but in every other aspect of my life I would have been much the poorer. I have shared my life with some incredible felines and they in turn have introduced me to some wonderful members of the cat fancy, and I have forged lifelong friendships with people who have purchased kittens from me. Little did I realise all those years ago how my existence would change when I bought two Burmese kittens to breed from – that small decision has hugely enriched my life.

Chapter 4. Caring for Your Cat Throughout Its Life

The long awaited day has arrived and you can now take your kitten home. Always transport a kitten in a purpose built carrier; cardboard carriers are of very little use as kittens and cats can easily escape from them. It is most unwise to transport a kitten loose in the car as, should there be an accident, the kitten could easily bolt in terror. It should also be considered that a wriggly kitten, unsure of its surroundings, could flee under the foot pedals and jeopardise the safety of all the passengers. Below is information copied from one of the leaflets in the kitten pack that I give to all new owners which is designed to help the kitten settle in quickly.

"The following notes contain a few tips to help your new baby settle quickly in your home. This is a big day for your kitten as he has been uprooted from all the familiar sounds and smells he has grown up with, separated from his littermates and the people he knows and trusts. Cats are predators and hide stress very well so reassurance is most important. All kittens are individuals and behave differently when confronted by new experiences. Some will walk into their new home and completely take over; others may be afraid and want to hide. When you get your kitten home, initially it is sensible to restrict his range and to provide a safe hiding place where he can feel secure – an old cardboard box with an entrance hole cut out will suffice. If the kitten does hide, encourage him to play but be sure to let him have quiet time, particularly if there are other animals or young children in the house. Somalis are incredibly nosey and their curiosity will soon get the better of any initial timidity. It is not unusual for the kitten to cry at first; he is calling for his siblings and mother, so even on warm nights, it is sensible to put a hot water

bottle in the bed to act as a comforter. A cuddly toy and a loud, old fashioned alarm clock ticking regularly replicates a heartbeat and also works well. For the first few days, let your kitten keep the blanket he has been sent with as this smells of home and is a comfort.

Your kitten is used to a litter tray which is lined with newspaper and with a grit type litter placed on top. If you wish to alter the type of litter e.g. to a wood based product, ensure that you make the change gradually. Do not change the food the kitten has been used to as this can lead to dietary upsets. In the early days, keep a careful eye on the consistency of the stools as stress can lead to upset tummies. Should the motions become loose, feed more dry food, chicken and fish and reduce prepared wet feeds.

Your kitten will need to be neutered. It is advisable to wait until the kitten is settled in his new home and then to have him micro-chipped at the same time. The kitten will not need vaccinating again until 12 months have elapsed. He will have been treated for fleas and worms and will need a repeat dose in a month's time or as per the manufacturer's recommendations.

Between the ages of 5 and 7 months, the kitten will shed his baby teeth and the adult teeth will erupt. Usually this goes unnoticed, but sometimes the kitten will nibble on things and it is important to ensure there are no electric wires accessible for chewing. Once teething begins, it is beneficial to add a dental diet to the complete feed. We use Hills TD which is available from large pet stores and recommend that this is used throughout life to maintain healthy teeth and gums.

If you have any problems, or if there is anything you are not certain about, do not hesitate to get in touch with me. My phone has a messaging service and I play back my calls frequently. Even if all is well, please phone after about 10 days just to let me know that you and your kitten are happy. If, for any reason during the life of your cat, you are unable to continue to offer a home for him, please contact me. As a breeder, I consider myself morally responsible for the welfare of all the kittens I have bred throughout their lives. Now enjoy a long and happy relationship with your new family member."

Now you have the responsibility of a kitten, you will need to register with a local vet and also to send the transfer certificate to the GCCF (which will mean the kitten is registered to your ownership). The relationship that you and your kitten have with your vet will hopefully be long and happy but do remember that, whether through a Pet Insurance company or directly, you are paying a substantial amount for professional expertise and should you be unhappy about any aspect of your pet's treatment, there is always the option to change. The breeder is always there to help and give advice, but so too is the GCCF. To keep your kitten healthy and happy, it is essential that it receives the very best nutrition available and this is important for the duration of his life.

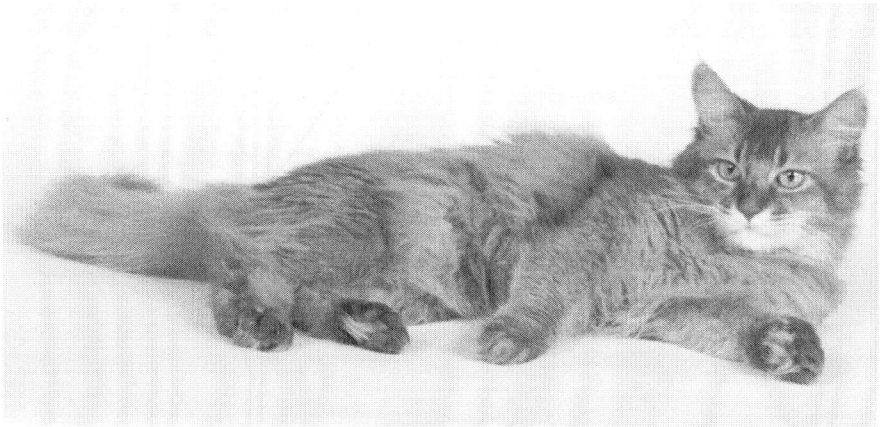

Below is a table of the essential dietary components.

Dietary component	
1) Water	Water is an essential part of the diet for cats and all mammals. Cats can get a lot of their water intake from eating moist food; hence canned food contains an average of 75% moisture. Cats do not have as high a thirst stimulus as dogs and this may be due in part to their desert dwelling ancestors. They are also predators and in the natural state would derive a high proportion of their fluid intake from their prey. (This is not uncommon with predators; I have a Barn Owl and like all raptors, she rarely needs to drink water as her prey provides her with sufficient intake. The water I give her is used for her daily bath!) An average cat requires approximately 60-80ml of water per kg of weight, depending upon weather and activity levels; a cat will drink more in warmer weather. A drop of approximately 10% in the water content of the body will result in dehydration. If there is a deficiency in the amount of water, the cat has a higher risk of developing urinary tract stones. If feeding dry food to a cat with a weak thirst drive, it is advisable to add water to the kibble. I have not encountered cats who drink excessively unless there is an underlying clinical condition, so excess water consumption is a good guide to the health of the cat and can be indicative of the onset of such diseases as diabetes or renal failure.
2) Proteins	Proteins are essential and they provide the material for muscle building, tissue repair and are the main source of energy. The daily amount required for a cat in its diet is a minimum of 29%, but most good quality dry feeds contain

	at least 33%. Dietary protein contains 10 specific amino acids that cats cannot manufacture themselves. A deficiency in any one of the essential amino acids can lead to serious health problems. Taurine is essential for cats and a deficiency can cause numerous problems, one of which is blindness. Arginine is essential as it removes ammonia in the urine from the body and a deficiency can cause a toxic build-up of ammonia in the blood stream. If cats are fed excess protein, as a rule this will be excreted in the urine or will be used for fuel, doing no harm to the healthy cat, BUT care should be taken when feeding protein to cats who have damaged kidneys.
3) Fats	Dietary fats provide the most concentrated source of energy. They make food more palatable and provide fatty acids which are carriers for soluble vitamins such as vitamins A, D, E, and K. Fatty acids play an important role in the structure and function of cells. The maximum amount of fat in the cat's diet can be reasonably high without any adverse effects. In many cat foods, 50% or more of the energy comes from fats. Essential fatty acids are needed to keep the cat's skin and coat healthy. A deficiency in fatty acids can lead to an impaired nervous system and can cause vision problems. Excess of fat in the diet can lead to obesity so intake should be carefully monitored. Diets high in fat are very palatable.
4) Vitamins	Vitamins are involved in many processes in the body and often work in conjunction with minerals and enzymes. Vitamins are divided in to 2 groups; fat soluble (A,D,E,K) and water soluble (B group and vitamin C). Fat soluble vitamins are stored in the liver and fatty tissues and released slowly, whereas water soluble vitamins are only stored in small quantities so a daily intake is required.

	Cats are able to synthesize Vitamin C.
	Vitamin A is fat soluble and found in the liver. Cats have to get all they need from the food they eat and a deficiency will have an adverse effect on the health of the eye. An excess of vitamin A can cause hypervitaminosis, a condition which is characterised by skeletal lesions. Vitamin D is a fat soluble vitamin and is responsible for maintaining the levels of calcium in the body; a deficiency can lead to rickets. An excess of vitamin D can lead to anorexia, lethargy and calcification of soft tissue.
5) Minerals	Minerals are essential for maintaining the health of the cat. Calcium and phosphorus are important for bone growth, whilst other minerals promote healthy skin, blood cells, and immune system. Most manufactured cat food comes already supplemented with minerals; these include calcium, phosphorus, magnesium and potassium - iron, copper, zinc and selenium are routinely added. Calcium is used for the formation of bones and teeth, among other things; a deficiency will cause loss of bone mineral content which can lead to collapse and curvature of the spine and pelvic bones. An excess of calcium can lead to decreased food intake, poor growth and calcification of the bones. Magnesium helps the mineral structure of the teeth and bones as well as having an effect on hormone secretion, muscle and nerve cell membrane stability. A deficiency would cause poor growth, convulsions and damage to the carpal joints. If magnesium is given in excess it can cause formation of stones in the urinary tract.

The Somali Cat

Not only is it important to ensure the cat has a daily intake of the dietary components but as cats are very fussy about how and where they eat, the following information about placement and serving food will make your feline's meal time a much better experience.

1) Do not put water and food bowls together; place them well away from the litter tray. Odour is a very important factor in a cat's life, and if the smell surrounding the food is not appealing, the cat will not eat.

2) Food and water bowls should be placed in a quiet area where the cat has a wide field of vision. In the natural state, the activity of feeding or drinking occurs when a potential predator could strike so if the cat feels threatened, it will become nervous and this will affect its wellbeing, both physically and mentally.

3) Make sure the food is served near to body temperature 38-39C. Food served from the fridge is not very palatable as the odour is diminished by chilling. If the food is warmed the odour is increased and therefore it will encourage the cat to eat. There is evidence to suggest that the smell of food is more important to the cat than the taste.

4) I serve food and water in stainless steel bowls which are much larger than those usually designated for cats which are sold in shops. Food can become tainted if plastic bowls are used; metal bowls wear better and do not degrade with disinfecting over time. Plastic bowls can emit odours which can be detected by the superior sense of smell common to cats. I use wide shallow bowls as some cats hate their whiskers touching the side of the bowl when eating; the whiskers are very sensitive and this can affect what should be a pleasurable experience.

5) Left to their own devices, cats are likely to eat between 10 -16 small meals a day. I let my cats graze on dry food over a twenty four hour

period; the amount offered is their daily allowance. Whilst some food is placed in the bowl, some is hidden away in various toys to mimic the hunting of the wild cat and to prevent boredom. I also feed wet food but this is not left down too long as it becomes dry and the odour then becomes unappealing to the cat.

The cat displays strong novelty behaviour where food is concerned; this is called neophilia - the desire to try foods not previously encountered. My own cats like a varied diet and enjoy trying new foods. On occasions, this has caught me out; having found a food they like and bought it in bulk, they will point blank refuse to eat it once I have crates of it in store! This is the monotony effect. Eating a variety of foods can be beneficial as it reduces the likelihood of an imbalanced diet. The development of food preferences in cats is very complex and not fully understood. Most cats prefer to consume a variety of foods but there are some who will develop a strong preference for one type of food. This may be the result of the owner buying a restricted group of foods or, alternatively, kittens can be influenced by their mother's food preferences. If cats are used to a constant diet this can cause problems when changing to a different variety. For this reason I make a point that all my kittens have a varied diet and stress the importance of this with their new owners. The introduction of a new food might cause a temporary increase in food consumption but any new food will have to be palatable and appeal to the cats' sense of smell.

Below is an example of the diet sheet I give all new owners when they purchase a kitten from me.

The kitten has eaten all the foods listed below whilst in our care. The quantities given are a guide as all kittens are individuals. Please remember not to place feed and water bowls near the litter tray; cats are very sensitive to scents. Water and food bowls should be sited away from each other and the best type of bowls to use are shallow stainless steel so that the whiskers do not touch the sides of the bowl.

Breakfast: 2ozs of cooked chicken/ mince / rabbit.

Lunch: 2ozs of white cooked fish / tuna in spring water / pilchards in tomato sauce.

Tea: 2ozs of prepared food i.e. Felix kitten / Iams kitten / Classic / Kitekat

Supper: 1 oz of complete feed. We have fed Taste of the Wild which is a grain free diet. Do introduce dried foods which help promote good dental hygiene e.g. Hills TD, and also use dried foods which help to reduce hairballs. Please remember the food you feed can ensure your cat has a long and healthy life.

On average a kitten needs 4 meals a day until 6 months of age when this can be reduced to 3 meals daily. By the time the cat is an adult (9 -12 months old), these should be reduced to 2 meals daily, following the manufacturer's guidelines as to quantity.

DO NOT give your kitten pasteurised milk as cats do not tolerate it; however, they can digest the specific brands of cat milk on the market. Do not feed a kitten adult Whiskas as this can cause upset stomachs as it is too rich. Water should be available at all times and changed daily.

Treats may be given but only in moderation; an obese cat has a shortened life expectancy and we all know how easy it is to pile on the pounds and how difficult it is to remove them!

Below is a table of the nutritional requirements for each life stage.

Life-stage:	Nutritional requirements:
Life-stage 1: Kittens (0-6 months)	For approximately 3 weeks the kittens get all their nutritional needs from their mother but weaning should start at 3-4 weeks of age. Kittens should be fed a diet high in calorific value as they need around 3 times more calories than an adult cat. The food should be high in protein with necessary other nutrients present so a good quality kitten food should be fed. Typically, a dry kitten food should have a protein content of 30%-40% and this high protein constituent is necessary for the rapid growth rate of kittens and for the development of a healthy body. Bone growth in kittens is rapid and calcium and phosphorus is necessary but care must be taken not to give too much as this can lead to problems such as calcification. A good quality balanced diet should cater for all their needs.
Life-stage 2: Junior (7mths -2 years)	The kitten is still growing although not as rapidly and is very active. Kitten food should be fed to meet the energy demands until kittens are approximately 8 months old when adult food can be introduced gradually. During this age span, the kitten will be neutered, which has the effect of slowing the metabolism and lowering the activity levels. There is a danger that the cat will gain weight which could lead to obesity if unchecked. Therefore, the ideal diet is one with high protein content but reduced fat.

Life-stage 3: Prime (3-7 years)	The nutritional requirements for this age group do not alter much but as the activity levels reduce each year constant monitoring of the weight is needed. Using high quality feeds will also reduce the risk of the onset of conditions to which this age group can be prone e.g. urinary tract disease and periodontal disease.
Life-stage 4: Mature (7-10 years)	The major problem with this age group is obesity; constant monitoring of body weight and adjustment of food intake accordingly is essential. The older cat is less able to digest fat and to a certain extent this applies to proteins also. A high protein diet of good quality is best as it is highly digestible. With high quality protein feeds, the phosphorus intake is restricted, helping to maintain renal function - renal failure is frequently seen in mature cats.
Life-stage 5: Senior (11-14 years)	Cats in this age group, unlike the mature stage, often have an increased energy requirement and therefore need an increased protein level to help maintain a lean body mass. They may struggle to absorb nutrients from their food and they have a tendency to lose weight. For this age group, I always add supplements weekly to their food to ensure the vitamin and mineral requirements are maintained
Life-stage 6: Geriatric (> 15 years)	The geriatric cat will incur the same problems seen in the senior age group, but more severely. They tend to suffer from low body mass and the ability to digest fat and protein will continue to reduce, so good quality, easily digested foods which are high in protein should be offered at

	more frequent intervals. Care should be taken with cats that are suffering from renal problems when feeding a high protein diet but for those whose kidney function is not impaired, high protein intake is necessary and phosphorus content still needs to be restricted.
Life-stage7: Pregnancy and lactation	Pregnancy makes huge nutritional demands and the calorie intake will increase through pregnancy; not only are you feeding the queen but also supporting the growth of the unborn kittens. To achieve this, it is advisable to feed kitten food throughout pregnancy and lactation. The amount of food fed should be gradually increased so that by the time the kittens are born, the cat will be consuming nearly double her normal daily intake. (This amount is variable with the size of the litter. I have found that when a queen is carrying only 1 or 2 kittens, she requires less; you do not want the cat to become fat as this can lead to problems at the birth, just as it does for overweight humans. A queen carrying a large litter will need more and as the pregnancy develops, she will need smaller meals more frequently because her distended uterus will limit the capacity of her stomach. The real clue to feeding a pregnant cat cannot be found in a text book; it is quite simply 'Know your queen'). A lactating queen has not only to feed herself but also her growing kittens, so the strain on her body is immense. A queen needs 3 times her normal intake of food once the kittens reach 4 weeks. It is best to feed ad lib dry high quality kitten food

which should also contain moderate levels of calcium as too much calcium is dangerous. Most queens will lose weight whilst nursing their kittens, however good the food you offer. (Over the years I have found my most diligent queens lose some body weight and some lose weight rapidly. In old fashioned terms, this is called 'milking off the back' and for this reason, I am a strong advocate of a queen only producing one litter a year which gives the body time for complete recovery. This is a personal belief as governing bodies allow 2 litters a year)

Feeding your cat is only a part of life care; cats also benefit from grooming. Somalis should be groomed daily and when you take your kitten home it will already be used to being groomed. Grooming should be fun and an enjoyable experience. Nearly all of my cats queue up when I bring out the combs and the breeder should show you which types of brushes and combs are most suitable for this breed. The Somali coat is soft and silky and because of this does not knot easily; regular grooming will keep the coat in pristine condition. During grooming is the ideal time to check for any wounds or lumps and you can also make sure there are no fleas present in the coat. Check the ears to see that they are clean and free from wax. It is good practise to get the kitten used to having his mouth opened. This will make it easy to check the state of the teeth and if, at any time, they need to take tablet medication it will not be a battle royal! Cats that lead an indoor existence will need to have their nails trimmed and this also applies to very elderly cats, even if they are allowed to free roam. All my kittens are used to this procedure before they leave me and I show the new owners how to clip the claws.

Once you have your kitten home, spend time interacting with him and provide plenty of toys. Over the years I have spent a fortune on the latest cat toys on the market yet the most successful toys have always been a cardboard box, brown paper bags and ping pong balls. Always supply a scratching post as this will help to save your furniture and wallpaper; please note I said "help to save"! Cats love to climb and jump, so do provide resting places at different levels. My own cats have a huge scratching post with lots of hidey holes which the manufacturers call the Cattullus because it is like a castle and they also adore their play tunnels. I use a lot of special balls which can be filled with dry food and as they play with them, the kibbles drop out. These toys provide an essential hunting aspect to life of which the indoor cat is deprived. My cats also like any stick with feathers but they don't have feathers for very long! These are great toys but the cat must not be left unsupervised with them. My cats also enjoy chasing laser lights but this toy should only be used for short periods of time since it can frustrate the cat as the chase never ends in the prey being caught.

Always be aware of the safety of your cat. I do not let my cats roam free as my back garden is fenced and roofed so they can play in the garden if they wish. Should you let your cat out, NEVER let it remain out at night as a cat is at its most vulnerable in the dark; it is advisable to call it in before dusk, when the smells of the wild are at their most enticing. There are many dangers in the home; cats are inquisitive and will happily climb into washing machines and tumble dryers, so make sure that doors on the machines are kept closed. Cats will also climb up chimneys so do block off access. There are other hazards in the home; some plants are highly toxic to cats (such as lilies and poinsettias) so do always check that any plants or flowers are safe around cats, who might happily nibble leaves with possibly fatal consequences. Anti-freeze and Jeyes fluid are lethal if ingested. Cats are highly susceptible to phenol based disinfectants; as a rough rule of thumb, if the disinfectant turns milky when water is added, take extreme care. Do not allow a cat near it until completely dry and do not use on food bowls.

With good nutrition, regular grooming, annual vet check-ups, and quality time interacting with your cat, you should have a very long, loving relationship between human and feline – enjoy.

Chapter 5. Showing your Cat

Your little Somali has now settled into your home and you are besotted; you think it is the best cat in the world. What could be better than showing everyone else the stunning beauty of your cat by taking up a new hobby and entering the world of showing cats? At a show you are guaranteed to share your day with likeminded people, all mad about their cats. The breeder will be only too willing to help you along the way; I always try to accompany people new to the show scene for their first outing, but here are some helpful hints as you embark on your new hobby.

You need to plan ahead; the GCCF has a list of shows, with the date, venue and details of the Show Manager. Write to the Show Manager requesting a schedule and enclose a large stamped addressed envelope. Read the schedule carefully; it should contain all the information you require but, if you are in doubt, contact the breeder or the Show Manager for help. Your entry fee will include entry to the Breed Class and some side classes but when a cat is new to being shown, it is always advisable not to enter too many classes; 3 or 4 classes is ample, and however tempting it is when you get the 'show bug', take it gently and do not enter your cat in too many shows. Show day should be a pleasant experience for cat and owner and you need to let your cat become accustomed to shows gradually.

In order to complete the entry form, you will need all your cat's details which can be found on the registration certificate. It is very wise to refer to this when filling in the form to ensure there are no spelling errors. Make sure you sign the form; you can also order extra admission tickets and a catalogue (which will usually be cheaper than it would be on show day). Include a stamped addressed envelope as confirmation that your entry has been received and accepted. Mistakes can happen in show administration and this is your proof on show day that your cat has been entered.

In advance of the show, you need to think how you are going to groom your cat; different breeders have differing techniques, so once again ask your breeder for advice; now you can see how important it is that your breeder will mentor you. Have a few trial runs at different methods of grooming because one method may suit your cat's coat better than another. In most cases, I bran bath my cats because most cats do enjoy this experience and some find a wet bath daunting (and so do the owners!) For a bran bath, you will need about 500 grams of broad leaf bran which can be bought from health shops. Place the bran in the microwave for 1 minute until it is warm; it should not be too hot to handle as this will cause burns to the cat. Now the fun begins; after many years experience, I have found it best either to bran bath the cat in a completely dry sink or to put the bran in a clean pillow case. Once the bran is ready rub it through the cat's coat, paying particular attention to areas where the coat is greasy as the bran will absorb any grease. When done in the sink, the bran can be swept up easily and if you use a pillow case, put the cat in the pillow case backwards so that only the head is free, then rub the bran through the coat.

Should you try putting the cat on newspaper and then rubbing the bran through the coat, believe me, you will be clearing up bran for a week. My cats love their bran baths, rolling luxuriantly through the warm bran. Brush the excess bran out of the coat; it won't all come out which is why it needs to be done the day before the show so that any small pieces will drop out during the day and will have all disappeared by show morning. If you decide to give a wet bath, the sooner you get the cat used to this method the better. There are many brands of shampoo on the market suitable for cats but make sure you do not use any products with colouring agents as this could mean your cat would be disqualified; for the same reason, there should not be powder in the coat.

Apart from the cat, there are certain things you will need to take to the show. Acceptance of entry, vaccination certificate, white litter tray, plain white blanket (not Cellular), white food dish (and food) and water bowl. I always take my own water to the show as my cats are used to it. You will also need to take your grooming kit. If you forget anything, don't worry as you can always purchase show kits at the show.

On arrival at the show you will be handed an envelope which will include your prepaid admission tickets and catalogue voucher. On the envelope will be your name, cats name, pen number, classes entered and a place for the vet's signature. Do not lose this envelope as it will be required as proof of ownership if you have to collect any prizes. You will then join the vetting in queue. One of the most nerve racking moments at a show for the owner is vetting in. You will be directed to a table with a vet and steward; put your carrier on the table and take your cat out. I prefer to use top loading carriers as it is much easier to remove the cat and is less stressful for them than front loading carriers; some cats can put the brakes on and I have seen exhibitors having to dismantle a carrier in order to remove their cat. Cats are examined by a vet on arrival to ensure that none are admitted into the show with a contagious disease. It is a good idea to get your cat used to having it's mouth opened and it's ears inspected. Vets check for fleas and if any are found, the cat will be refused entry. The ears are checked; they should be clean and there should be no evidence of ear mites. There should be no nasal or ocular discharge and the eyes should be bright, not sore or watering; if there is any suspicion of infection anywhere on your cat, you will not be admitted. Never show a cat with any wounds or bald patches as these can be indicative of ringworm; this will involve you in lengthy and costly procedures so leave the cat at home. When the vet is satisfied the cat is fit, he will sign your vetting in slip and you can then enter the hall.

Find your pen and disinfect it; pens are cleaned between shows but it is always wise to use wipes which are non-toxic to cats, just to make sure. Put the blanket and litter tray in the pen and then put the cat in. If the journey has been a long one, the cat will need to use the tray so the quicker you can get the cat into the pen, the better. Give the cat some water; the best bowls are those which have hooks and can be attached to the wire of the pen; place the bowl at the back of the pen. You can also feed your cat but do not be surprised if the cat doesn't eat; some are reluctant to do so at shows. You must remove the feed bowl before judging commences at 10am. Do any final grooming that may be necessary.

When the main judging commences, you will be asked to leave the hall; at some shows you can still walk around the stalls which sell a variety of cat related items but you must not walk around the judging area. On your way out of the hall you will be able to obtain a catalogue. Check your cat is entered in the right classes, and the name is spelt correctly; if there are any mistakes see the Show Manager straight away. You will be allowed to return to your cat at lunchtime, give him a cuddle, feed him and if necessary tidy the pen. The rest of the afternoon is spent looking after your cat, chatting to friends and waiting for results. Not all the classes will have been judged so if you see a judge approaching your pen move some distance away. Judges are very approachable and will discuss your cat with you; however, do not speak to a judge or identify your cat in any way until they have finished all their judging for the day, or your cat may be disqualified.

In, or adjacent to, the hall there will be a results board; look for the number of the class and then find your cat's number and see what is written beside it. If there is nothing, it means your cat was unplaced. In Breed classes, rosettes are awarded for 1st, 2nd and 3rd and your cat may also be awarded Best of Breed. At the bottom of the results slip it will usually say BOB and the number of the cat that has gained the award. If your cat is eligible for a certificate, PC (Premier Certificate) or CC (Challenge Certificate) will be written by its pen number. A certificate signed by the judge will be placed on your pen towards the end of the show.

You are not allowed to remove your cat from the show before it closes, unless you have permission from the Show Manager – this is usually only given in exceptional circumstances. In over thirty years of showing and having attended hundreds of shows, I have only asked twice to leave a show early; once, when I had a very sick cat at home that needed time sensitive medication and very recently when my road was being closed off for a huge firework display. I have been very lucky over the years of showing; many of my cats have achieved the title of Champion, Grand Champion, Imperial and UK Grand Champion and the Premier equivalents.

I still remember the first time one of my cats made Champion; it was not on the result board but the rosettes were on his pen and despite all my friends wanting to celebrate, I refused until I saw it in print - then did we party! My first Grand Champion was at The Abyssinian Show; what a day! I bought a bottle of Champagne and we all had a few sips to celebrate. The first rosette I won in 1980 still has pride of place on my wall although it is looking a bit tired now; the rosettes of today are far superior in quality but for me, it signifies the start of an incredible hobby.

Showing is a hobby; it should be fun and a good day out. Judges work hard all day and their work does not stop when they have finished judging; they must then return home and write reports on the cats that they have judged. Remember; the judge can only please one person in a class and that is the winner. The same cat judged by two individuals can get differing results, because at the end of the day judges are only human and they have their personal preferences. When I started showing, a very senior judge told me that a winning show cat was 95% excellence and 5% showman and this is so true; in a close run contest, the cat who shows off the most will invariably catch the judge's eye. Some years ago, I was lucky enough to have bred two cats that were being judged for Overall Best in Show. Queenie behaved impeccably but made no effort to win the judge's heart. Earl, my son's cat, was not of such a good standard but as the judge was making her decision, Earl raised his paw as if to say 'Give it to me'. The crowd responded with 'aahs' and it was a done deal; the judge's heart melted and Earl won Overall Best in Show exhibit. I was pleased that he had won but was doubly thrilled as my son, then in his twenties, let out a whoop of joy and punched the air with delight; even as a grown man, to my son, Earl was the best cat ever.

The Somali Cat

Over the years I have experienced some fraught moments whilst pursuing my hobby. We have had some very interesting train journeys and nearly been stranded overnight on a snow bound motorway. Staying overnight in hotels with cats is not always plain sailing as the following story illustrates. One year, I had a litter of Somalis born on April 1st and I decided to give them names appropriate to April Fools Day. One was called Harlequin and the other named Joker. They were a delightful pair and were soon booked by an elderly couple, Colin and Jo Hubert. I had entered them for a show and it was agreed that I could keep them until the show had taken place. I set off from home with the two cats and my son and daughter. We had decided to make a weekend of it and had booked into The Moathouse Hotel in Chester. The hotel was aware I was bringing cats and I was delighted upon entering the room to find that a cat bed had been prepared for them.

I was looking forward to a relaxed evening and a slap up meal, all prepared and no washing up. I had checked the room very carefully to make sure the kittens could not escape before I let them out of their cat basket. Once we had all settled down, I decided to go and explore the facilities the hotel had to offer, leaving the kittens with my offspring. On returning to the room, I thought it best to give the kittens a grooming session but they were nowhere to be seen. At this stage I didn't panic; kittens can hide in the tiniest of places and it was just a matter of carefully searching every nook and cranny in the room. We upturned beds, pulled out drawers and searched the wardrobes but all to no avail; a cold feeling began to creep over me when my son, David, shouted from the bathroom to come and look. The bathroom had marble effect tiling but under the hand basin there was a gap of about three inches. Relief flooded over me; obviously the kittens had crawled behind the panel and as luck would have it, David had his Swiss Army knife on him with all manner of gadgets attached. In a matter of minutes the panel was removed but the sight which greeted me was not what I expected; instead, terror gripped me. The kittens were not there but what was worse, all I could see was a vast expanse of darkness.

By now I was like a woman possessed, the kittens were lost and their new owners were expecting to take them to their new home in a few days time. I ran to reception and told them what had happened. The manager came with me to the room which by now closely resembled a war zone with bed overturned, drawers discarded haphazardly and my son dismantling everything in sight with his Swiss Army knife. He made no comment about the state of the room (I'm sure partly due to the fact that he thought he was dealing with an unstable woman) but he did say the black hole which confronted us was a fire safety measure which encircled the entire third floor of the hotel. Even worse, he couldn't guarantee that the kittens would not be able to escape on to the roof. Drastic measures were called for; the Maintenance Manager (who had left work early to attend a party) was called back to work and the plans of the hotel were pored over intensely. Access to the loft area was through small doors, so systematically we worked through the rooms, calling the kittens and shining spotlights into the abyss; finally the light picked up the eyes of a kitten and my son, who was small enough, valiantly crawled in to the space and retrieved the kittens one by one. I have never been so glad to see kittens, but they were a sorry sight. Their whiskers were draped in cobwebs and their coats covered in all manner of dust. The entire evening was spent trying to remove the debris from their coats. When we left the hotel the following morning, everyone wanted to see the delinquents who had caused so much chaos. To this day, I shall always be indebted to the staff of this hotel - but the story does not end there. Once at the show they performed like true Somalis, winning their classes and they were the talk of the show. Towards the close of the show, the Show Manager came and spoke quietly to me; a judge had found a flea on Joker but, considering his experience, they would not take any further action. I was not surprised - it's amazing they did not find cobwebs! They duly went to their new owners who called them Harley and Jo Jo and they were much loved pets; many years later I would discover what an impact my two mischievous imps had on their doting owners.

I have mentioned the sterling work of the judges but not that of Show Managers. Again, they are volunteers and dedicate many hours of hard work to produce a show. I do believe that all exhibitors should get involved in running a show and then they may have some comprehension of all the hard work that goes into the day. Show Managers do their very best to please everyone; it is a long day for them, with months of preparation necessary. They are the unsung heroes of the Cat Fancy and a word of thanks to them at the end of the show is much appreciated.

To sum up: showing should be an opportunity to meet friends and if you are lucky enough to win, enjoy the success and if you lose, be graceful in defeat. Remember, you brought the best cat to the show and regardless of what anyone else thinks, you are taking the best cat home again at the end of the day.

Chapter 6. Genetics and Breed Selection

Anyone wishing to breed cats should have an understanding of basic genetics. There are hundreds of books written purely about genetics so in this chapter I will endeavour to cover the basics which concern the Somali breed.

All cats have 38 chromosomes. Every cell contains two copies; one from the sire and one from the dam. The sperm and egg cell only contain a single copy; when the egg is fertilised, these two cells then combine into a single cell containing copies, half from the mother and half from the father. Each chromosome is one long strand of a single molecule of DNA. Of the 38 chromosomes (19 pairs) that are in each cell, 36 are referred to as AUTOSOMES and these are the same in both sexes. The last two are sex chromosomes (X or Y) which determine the gender of the cat. Females have two X chromosomes in each cell, other than' the egg cell which contains a single X chromosome. Males have one X chromosome and one Y chromosome in their non-sperm cells. In the sperm cells, one half of the cells produced by the sire contain an X chromosome and the other half contain a Y chromosome. For this reason, it is the sire who determines the gender of the kitten.

The longhaired Somali is always a ticked tabby cat with the basic genotype AA, ll, ss,Ta.

GENOTYPE is the cat's complete genetic identity. AA means they are HOMOZYGOUS for the agouti allele ('homo' is from the Greek and means 'same') and I will explain in simple terms what this means. Homozygous means that there are two identical copies of a gene. The agouti gene is responsible for determining whether the coat is banded (agouti) or a solid colour (non agouti). Long hair Somalis have two copies of the long hair gene meaning that they breed true for long hair. Just to confuse the issue, this does not apply to Shorthaired Somalis who are HETEROZYGOUS for the longhaired allele, which means that they have dissimilar pairs of genes ('hetero' is from the Greek and means 'varied').

'ss' indicates that Somalis are homozygous for the non-white spotted allele of the white spotting gene, important because the Somali Standard of Points regards a white locket or any patches of white fur other than around the chin, nostrils and lips as a severe fault and all awards should be withheld at a show. Ta means that Somalis are homozygous for the ticked tabby pattern and all Somalis breed true for ticked tabby; no other patterns should be seen.

There are 28 different colours of Somalis and these variations in colour are controlled by a group of both dominant and recessive genes; consequently, one cannot fully understand colour inheritance in Somali cats without a basic understanding of cat genetics. Knowledge of whether a mutation is recessive or dominant is vital if breeding is to produce the desired colours. Included later in this book is a simple colour mating chart.

I would like to mention here the breeding of silver Somalis; all silver Somalis have one or two copies of the inhibitor (I) allele. This is dominant allele and suppresses the development of pigment in the hair of the coat, typically producing hair that is fully coloured only at the tip and has a silvery white base. When a silver cat is mated to a non-silver, one would expect the kittens to be 50% silver and 50% non-silver. Homozygous silvers will only be produced when both parents are silver and then only at the ratio of 1:4. Cats which are homozygous for silver (not carrying non-silver) will produce all silver kittens.

When you first begin breeding, I firmly believe that you should start with the basic colours – Usual, Sorrel, and Blue - and for this reason, I am not going to write about sex linked Somalis who can produce any number of colours; experience is needed to determine what colour they are. Breeders register their kittens and they must ensure that the colour of each kitten is correctly registered. There are now DNA tests available for some colours which can be used for clarification but, should there be any doubt about the colour of a kitten, it is not of the desired quality to be bred from or shown.

The breeder should draw up a list of criteria when deciding from which cats to breed. There are various selection methods.

Firstly, PHENOTYPE; this is a description of actual physical characteristics such as size, colour, behaviour and general disposition. Phenotype is influenced by genotype (nature) and environment and upbringing (nurture). Phenotype selection is based solely upon the evaluation of external characteristics.

Secondly, GENEALOGICAL selection, which is based on knowledge of the cat's ancestors and is only effective where there is complete information about related cats, which is not always available.

Thirdly, GENOTYPE selection; this is based on the evaluation of the cat's descendants. First time breeders can only select by phenotype until the number of offspring is sufficient, when genotype selection is possible. This maintains the continuation of good Somali breed type already achieved, whilst giving scope to further improve aspects of type, coat, pattern and colour and to meet the ideal described in The Standard of Points.

Three key rules should be followed.

1. Health is paramount and should be the most important consideration. It should be monitored constantly and any evidence of weakness or lack of vigour should be dealt with immediately. Many years ago, when Somalis were first bred in the UK, we had dental problems resulting in early loss of teeth and gingivitis but now this issue has largely been addressed through selective breeding.

2. The good and bad features of the individual cats should be assessed and weighed against each other before mating. To enable this assessment, it is good practice to show your cat and learn from the judges where the cat may fall short of the breed standard. For example, if the cat has a short tail you would not use a stud with the same fault. The breeding of cats with similar faults should be avoided at all costs as there is a danger of fixation (homozygosis).

3. When planning a breeding programme, breeders must realise that doubling the good traits in a cat could also result in doubling the defects. There are no short cuts to good breeding; a breeding programme is not a programme for the next litter or the next year. When I embark upon a programme, I expect it to take between five and ten years before I have reached the goals I have set to achieve the breeding I desire.

To sum up; when I am evaluating a kitten to retain for future breeding, or to sell for breeding, I adhere to the following criteria of which all must be met.

Ask yourself how close the kitten is to the Standard of Points and consider the number of faults he has. No one has bred the perfect cat and I doubt they ever will; some faults are minor, such as a slightly shorter tail. If the kitten was excellent in every other respect I would allow that fault.

Other faults are major, such as skeletal deformities e.g. I would not breed from a kitten with an uneven bite.

The temperament of the kitten is vital and I would never breed from either a male or female with a suspect temperament. The health of the kitten and of the parents is also paramount. Sometimes, particularly with experience, you get a gut feeling that the kitten has just got that special something; they call it breeders intuition.

Throughout this chapter I have referred to the Standard of Points, a detailed account of which can be found later in the book. However, here I would like to give a guide to the general standard for Somalis. The Somali Standard of Points is the bible for all Somali breeders. It calls for a balanced cat of medium build and foreign type. A Somali should demonstrate style and elegance with a lithe and muscular body and it should have long slender legs with neat, oval tufted paws. The head should be broad, forming a moderate wedge with gently rounded contours. The muzzle should also be rounded and generous to give the unique Somali smile. The eyes are large and almond shaped with an oblique aperture and set well apart. The eye colour may be green or yellow/gold. The Somali profile should show a slight nose break, the chin should be firm and the neck elegant. All Somalis have dark rims to the eyes surrounded by lighter spectacles. This highlights and accentuates the size of the eyes, making them most expressive and appealing. The ears should be set wide apart, but not low, and be broad at the base, proportionately large, pricked and well cupped. The longhair Somali should have tufted ears which are also well furnished. The tail should be long and tapering with a full brush. A Somali's expression should be alert and smiling; any suggestion of a pinched, 'snipey' look should be severely penalised by judges on the show bench. A Somali should be in excellent condition with good weight and muscle tone for its size.

Throughout this chapter I have mentioned genetic testing; every day new discoveries are being made. All breeders should be aware there are genetic anomalies; this does not mean that they are common but cats will have a quota of defects, just as are found in all other species. There is a genetic disorder that is known to affect Somalis called Erythrocyte Pyruvate Kinase Deficiency (PK Def). This is an inherited haemolytic anaemia that occurs in Abyssinians, Somalis and other breeds. There is a deficiency in an enzyme which causes an instability of red blood cells leading to anaemia. The anaemia is intermittent, the age of onset is variable and so are the clinical signs. This is an inherited condition and is one that is very close to my heart; as you read on you will discover why.

During the nineties, Somali breeders were concerned that a number of Somalis were suffering from liver related problems such as jaundice and anaemia but there was no known cause and vets were unable discover the causal agent. It led to the premature death of some Somalis. As breeders, we knew something was not quite right but were at a loss as to how to solve the problem. Then, in 2000, my queen Kizzie gave birth to a litter of kittens. There were five of them but the last kitten to be born (a cream male) was very reluctant to breathe. I resuscitated him but he was very cold and refused to suckle. To retain his body heat, I wrapped him in a tinfoil jacket and administered first life drops and colostrum. The next day, he had improved and within days he was as bonny as his littermates. Already I had a soft spot for this tiny little soul and referred to him as my little Cracker; there was no better name for him. When Cracker was thirteen weeks old, he was due to go to a new home, but in a play fight with his brother his eye was damaged entailing an emergency trip to the vet. Then began weeks of treatment to save the eye; it was clear he would be going nowhere soon and my vet said it could be months before the eye was healed, so I decided that Cracker would stay with me. As he was young, the eye healed quickly and by the time he was a year old all the scarring had disappeared.

Cracker was a typical Somali; he was a perfect patient and an absolute character. His one passion in life was a cup of tea. Anyone who had a cuppa in our house would have to fight him off as he would have his head in the cup before you could blink. I lost count of the number of cups he overturned to get at his favourite tipple. He was very mischievous and was one of the very few cats I have had who preferred to sharpen his claws on the wallpaper rather than the scratching post. His favourite piece of wallpaper was outside my bedroom at the top of the stairs. Then, when Cracker had just celebrated his first birthday, disaster struck.

When I feed my cats first thing in the morning, they all come rushing from every direction for their breakfast. On this particular morning, Cracker remained on the rug by the fire, showing no interest in food. I picked him up and nothing seemed obviously wrong until I opened his mouth and saw that all the membranes were white; Cracker was anaemic. An emergency trip to the vet did not help to allay my fears; she was guarded in her prognosis, blood tests were taken and we awaited the results. These were not good news; in layman's terms, Cracker had a condition in which his own immune system had turned in on itself, destroying the red blood cells. He was given massive doses of steroids and antibiotics to fight any secondary infection and then began one of the most intensive nursing sessions I have ever experienced with a cat. I never left his side - where I went Cracker, went also. He was so weak he could not walk, so I carried him around with me in the slings which are used for babies. He wouldn't eat, so all food was either pureed or a specialised convalescent veterinary diet which I fed to him from a syringe. There were many times in those early days when I thought I would lose him; once when his nose began to bleed and again when he urinated blood; all signs that he was haemorrhaging. The worst time was when he was gasping for breath one night; his red blood cell count was so low that the oxygen was struggling to get round his body. I felt completely helpless then and expected him to slip away that night, but in fact, it was the turning point; somehow his body survived and very slowly he began to recover. He started to eat for himself; chicken breast and rabbit were his favourites. He began to walk; just short distances and then he would flop, exhausted from the effort. I had a very simple way of gauging his recovery; he always came to bed with me and at first he would sit on the bottom stair waiting for me to carry him up. Then it would be step two and so on. I knew Cracker was back on form the day he raced past me on the stairs, got to the top and started scratching the wallpaper. I have never been so pleased to see a cat vandalise the house!

Once again, Cracker was his usual self - climbing up my back, perching on my shoulder, grooming me, drinking his tea and dancing. Yes, Cracker loved music and would stand on his hind legs with his paws on my knees and he would dance. However, I knew whilst Cracker lived his life would not be plain sailing. He had to have regular blood tests which he really hated, although he never raised a claw but he wriggled for England. His medications and dosages were always under review and I knew from the outset that the drugs he needed to survive would eventually kill him with long term usage. Every day we had together was a bonus; there were not many of his nine lives left in the bank.

While Cracker made his recovery, I noticed that the tip of his tail and the tips of his ears looked bent. On a visit to the vet I brought this to her attention; I wasn't really bothered by the bent bits but I was puzzled. My vet calmly said that part of his tail would eventually drop off and so too would the ear tips as the extremities had been starved of oxygen when Cracker had been fighting for breath. As the weeks went by, this duly happened but Cracker seemed unperturbed by it. Now that he was living the life of a normal cat once again, I turned my mind to what had caused his illness because every vet had said the condition was extremely rare. I did a lot of research and found that in America, a gene had been discovered which caused fragility of the red blood cell wall.

The Somali Cat Club committee started to research the condition and within the next two years found that it was named (PK Def) and also that there was a genetic test available in the States. The Club worked closely with Andrea Harvey from Langford and after raising £1000 to pay for testing, we began to eradicate the rogue gene. Test results showed that the gene had been present right from the beginning in the cats imported from America. Fortunately, it was easy to eradicate. In the Normal status, the gene was not present, in the Carrier status there was one copy of the gene which would have no effect on the cat's health and finally, in the Affected status, there were two copies of the gene which would be likely to cause health problems. The best mating to perform is normal to normal but normal can be mated to carrier as, in the worst case scenario, this will only produce carrier cats; in the early days, we had no option but to do this. The reason was that we only had a small gene pool and to remove a number of cats all at once from breeding lines could have created even greater problems in the future. Since the 24th October 2007, all Somalis registered with the GCCF on the active register are screened for the gene.

It came as no surprise to me when I tested Cracker that he was an affected cat. However, in his own way he became quite famous. He was selected for an award as one of the bravest cats in Great Britain because of his courage in coping with all the veterinary treatment he had to undergo. As a result of that, he was asked to appear on a television programme which explored rare veterinary conditions. For five years after he first became ill, he led a normal, happy life doing all the things a Somali does. Over those years, I had learnt to notice the slightest change in his demeanour which invariably meant that the dosage of his medication needed to be adjusted. Not only did I know Cracker's every mood, he could also read me like a book and would respond to my moods. When I noticed Cracker was not his usual self, I also realised that this had nothing to do with his on-going condition; this was something different. My vet was away on holiday, so on her return a few days later I booked a consultation. My vet knew something was amiss as soon as I turned up and confirmed what I already suspected; Cracker had an inoperable intestinal tumour. He could have lived perhaps for a few weeks but he would have struggled and slowly been destroyed by the cancer. There was no choice; this was a battle neither of us could win and the kindest thing to do was to put him to sleep. Over the years I have lost many of my animal friends and I try to fight the tears back until I am out of the vet's surgery. This time it was impossible – I wept freely as I held him and talked to him as he was given the overdose of anaesthetic. I wasn't the only one in tears; Cracker had been a regular patient and his determination and character always shone through. My vet also wept for Cracker; it was the end of an incredible journey.

I don't remember the drive home, but Cracker was buried in my garden and, just as the Egyptians had done thousands of years ago, I buried a mug with him so he could have a cup of tea in the afterlife. The bond I had with Cracker was unique and I doubt I shall ever experience such an intense relationship with a cat again. Some years later, Cracker was posthumously awarded The Anne Rickson Trophy which is awarded annually by the Somali Cat Club for the cat who has contributed most to the breed. It was Cracker's illness which made me search for answers and in so doing, PK Def is now eradicated from the lines of responsible breeders. Writing Cracker's story has once again reduced me to tears; in memory of the wonderful times we shared, it is fitting that such a loving companion should have this book dedicated to him and to all the other Somalis who have been loved and lost.

Another genetic anomaly that is known to affect Somalis is Progressive Retinal Atrophy (PRA). This is a hereditary form of progressive degeneration of the rods and cones in the retina which can lead to blindness. At the time of writing, there have been no documented cases of blindness in Somali cats in the UK. There are different forms of PRA and the DNA tests available at the moment still need to be refined as recent research suggests there are some anomalies which can affect the results. The Somali Cat Club advises members to use the test if they are concerned about the potential for PRA in their lines to use the test and advises that imported cats should be tested.

In conclusion, Somalis in breeding programmes should be of show quality, pleasing type, correct colour and with well defined ticking. They should be affectionate and of sound temperament. A healthy, happy Somali is a joy to own.

Chapter 7. The Stud Cat and Mating Your Queen

When you decide to breed, it is my belief that you are about to experience one of the most fantastic hobbies there is. You should by now have shown your cat and be aware of her faults. At shows, you will have met other breeders, some of whom will own stud cats. You should have done your research, checked on the pedigrees and suitability of the stud for your queen. When I first began breeding, I read as many books as I could and my phone bill trebled overnight as I chatted to breeders, gaining as much helpful information as possible from their experience. Owning a stud cat is not for the novice breeder as you need to rely on the stud owner, among others, for advice. Owning a stud cat incurs great expense as the stud will need his own living quarters; entire males do not make good house cats as when they reach sexual maturity, they will spray indiscriminately to mark their territory. The urine of an entire male cat is one of the most pungent odours known to man!

All the studs I have bred and owned have begun life as kittens in the house. It is most important that your potential stud is well socialised as a kitten; there is bond between Stud cat and owner which is very different from your relationship with your queen. The stud must trust you and in turn, you must trust the stud. There will be times with a visiting queen when you will have to intervene in the mating process (some queens will roll over during mating and when this happens, the stud owner may have to hold the queen in position for the stud). If you have not built up a strong bond, the stud may take exception to your interference. Studs are powerful and far more unpredictable than neutered males, so care should always be taken.

The stud house will become your cat's kingdom and it should be spacious, close to the house, easy to keep clean and have plenty of furnishings such as scratching posts to keep him occupied. At the time of writing, I would not expect to build a suitable house for less than £1500 and this is just the beginning of your expenditure. The cat will need to be well fed throughout the year and you will incur routine veterinary fees. The life of a stud can be a lonely existence so it is imperative you spend time with your stud each day. When I first move my studs into their quarters, I do it gradually, alternating between the house and the stud pen and slowly increasing the time spent outside. Be prepared for your plan not to come to fruition as it takes certain particular characteristics for a cat to live happily as a stud. Over the years, I have neutered some wonderful examples of the breed because they did not like life as a stud; they preferred the fire side. An unhappy stud is of no use and neither is a stud with a bad temperament. A stud can do untold damage to future generations of the breed so he must be a superb example of the Standard of Points and have a temperament to match.

The stud owner has the added responsibility of caring for the visiting queen. Some queens will be very nervous and a great deal of time will need to be spent allaying their fears. They may be aggressive on arrival; others, having howled the house down, suddenly go right off the idea of sex and refuse to mate. When cats mate, it is a violent procedure and the stud can be injured; in order to prevent injury, you need to know exactly what you are doing. The stud owner should make every effort to keep the queen in the condition that she arrived in. Sometimes, this can be very difficult as some studs, particularly inexperienced ones, can scruff the queen too much and her neck will then become bald. When I began breeding, Somalis were not even available in the UK and my first stud was a Burmese who I called Bill. He was a wonderful stud who loved his ladies. Some years into his stud career, a friend asked if she could bring her Chinchilla queen to him. At that time a new breed was making its debut (the Burmilla) and this was produced by out-crossing Chinchillas to Burmese. I had seen some of these cats at shows and thought them very impressive so I was quite happy for Bill to be involved in pioneering the breed.

My friend duly arrived with her cat Minnie. I was unsure how Bill would react to this very longhaired, fluffy ball of cat but I need not have worried; as far as Bill was concerned, she was female and he was about to have some fun. They mated successfully during the day and usually I would have separated them at night, but my friend had told me that Minnie only called for about 36 hours, so that if they were happy, leave them together. I checked on them before I went to bed and all was well. The next morning one of the first things I did was to check on the honeymooners. You cannot begin to imagine my horror when I opened the cat flap to be greeted by Bill with his mouth full of silky Chinchilla hair. I wrenched the main door open and found the floor covered in hair; I did think for one awful moment that Bill had killed her but there, sitting dejectedly in the litter tray, was a very alive but naked Minnie! Throughout the night, Bill had systematically plucked all her fur leaving only her head and tail untouched; amazingly, there was not one mark on her flesh. Clearly, my boy wanted to turn her into a shorthaired cat.

I had no option but to phone my friend and tell her what had happened; she was none too pleased and arranged to fetch Minnie that morning. I went back to the stud house and swept up all the fur, placing it in a carrier bag and then musing over the fact Bill had probably ruined a good friendship with his antics. My friend duly arrived and I took her to Minnie. Her reaction was not what I expected; the sight of her naked queen reduced her to helpless fits of laughter. It was fortunate she could see the funny side of things and our friendship has remained intact to this day. And what of Minnie? She wasn't pregnant and never called again; her night of passion with Bill had put her off sex for life!

Before you take your queen to stud, the stud owner will have certain criteria that you must fulfil. There are documents that need to be taken with you, including your cat's pedigree and vaccination certificates. Should your queen be pregnant and become due for a booster vaccination during her pregnancy or while nursing, it is wise to have her boosted early so that she has maximum protection and can pass on her antibodies to her kittens. The queen should also be wormed and treated with a flea preparation before visiting the stud and her claws should be clipped. You will also need to take your GCCF registration certificate. The GCCF has two registers; the active and the non-active. A cat used for breeding must be on the active register in order that the progeny may be registered. The stud owner will need to see proof of this; it is a method of safeguarding the integrity of the breed by preventing inferior quality cats being bred from. No cat on the non-active register can be bred from. Never be afraid to ask to see the paperwork for the stud cat. He should be fully vaccinated and have a certificate of entirety meaning that he has been examined by a vet, both testicles are descended and that there are no apparent abnormalities in that department! The stud owner may ask for you to have certain blood tests done before your queen will be accepted; the most common test requested is for FeLV and FIV. The queen will be left with the stud, usually for at least three days. When you collect your queen, you will receive a mating certificate (proof of the sire of the litter) which must be sent with the litter application to the GCCF when you register the kittens. You will also be given a copy of the stud's pedigree and the approximate dates when the kittens are due. The stud fee charged is at the discretion of the owner but, as a rough guide, a stud fee is usually the same as the price of a pet quality kitten. The fee you pay is for the services of the stud, not on results. Most breeders will offer a second mating free of charge if the queen is not pregnant at the first attempt but do not assume this; ask the stud owner what their policy is.

Reproductive Anatomy
Cats are induced ovulators, which means that a mating must occur to induce ovulation. To enable ovulation after the stud has penetrated the queen, the penis has minute barbs which cause the queen pain as he withdraws which stimulates ovulation. It is possible for cats to be mated by two different males and kittens from both males can be born in a litter.

Reproductive Physiology
Cats are fertile creatures and if left to their own devices can produce 3 litters a year. My own cats have 1 litter a year; occasionally, for health reasons and the wellbeing of the cat, I may mate one sooner. The GCCF advises a maximum of two litters per year. The oestrus cycle is seasonal,

usually January to September, but my own female cats, who are kept indoors and live happily together, will breed all the year round. This is due to the fact that in a natural situation, the breeding season is dictated by the amount of light available; the longer the days, the more the sexual activity. My cats are house cats and have artificial light 14 hours a day; females living together will promote shared periods of oestrus. Oestrus behaviour in cats develops very suddenly, whereas in dogs there are clear signs of pro-oestrus. Bleeding in the cat does not occur but the vulva may be more moist than usual. The biggest change in the cat is their behaviour. The queen will become friendlier, rubbing up against things. They become more active, rolling on the floor and usually vocalising - to be exact, banshee wailing! I have had more than one phone call from owners distraught that their cat must have been poisoned because it is screaming in pain and rolling around; to date, it has never been anything more serious than an amorous female looking for a mate! They will also adopt the posture of crouching down on the front legs with the back legs extended and paddling. The tail is usually held stiffly to one side. If picked up, their body will become rigid rather than the more usual relaxed pose. Sometimes, they may visit the tray frequently, giving the signs of cystitis; this is further evidence of oestrus. Pro-oestrus lasts 1-2 days. This is followed by oestrus which can last 4-6 days if a male is present and up to 10 days if no male is present. The queen will accept the male and ovulation is induced. If the queen does not ovulate, she will begin her next cycle as soon as 10 days later. If the queen is pregnant, as a general rule the next cycle after the birth of the kittens will occur 3-4 months later. However, I have had queens who come into call when the kittens are only a few days old; fortunately, the majority do not call again until the kittens have left home.

Mating Behaviour

During mating, the tom bites the neck of the female and the penis (which usually faces backwards) once erect faces forward. Copulation is short; 30 seconds to 5 minutes. As the male dismounts, the queen gives a copulatory howl and the stud retreats, as the queen will attack him if he hangs around.

This is because the backward facing barbs on the penis scrape against the vagina triggering the release of hormones which in turn stimulate ovulation. The pain of withdrawal that makes the queen attack. In over 30 years of breeding, I have made sure that my inexperienced studs get well out of the way after mating; in order to do this, there must be a bond between stud and owner and each must have complete trust in the other. This is one of the reasons why stud work is so rewarding. Twenty four hours after mating, the sperm reaches the egg and fertilisation takes place. I usually run the queen with the stud for 3-4 days under supervision so there are multiple matings. I always advise owners not to move a queen to stud until the second day of oestrus as, if moved too early, they can go off call. In the same way, if a queen is mated after the 4th day of call, the chances of a successful mating diminish. In an ideal world, I do not mate a queen before she is a year old but the time of year that a female is born can dictate the timing of their first season. Most females will come into call from January onwards so, if they are born in September, you are faced with a four/five month old kitten in season. I always advise never to mate on the first season; try for the second or third. Do try not to go beyond the fourth call as the cycles can get closer together and the queen will appear to be in a perpetual state of oestrus which can cause loss of body condition and a successful mating becomes unlikely.

Mating Physiology

If the mating has been successful, the length of pregnancy is 63-65 days but the range can be as wide as 58-72 days, although in my experience any kittens born before 60 days have little chance of survival and I would not let any of my queens go past 67 days without consulting a vet. In a maiden queen, at 19 days the nipples will begin to enlarge and become very pink; in an established breeding queen this is evident later on, from day 21 onwards. Abdominal palpation can be done from 17-25 days or ultrasound can be used after 3 weeks.

During pregnancy, the queen gains weight from conception to parturition. In the early part of the pregnancy, the weight gain is due to increased fat stores which will be needed later on when she is lactating. Later in the pregnancy, the weight gain is due to size and weight of the foetuses. The uterus has two horns and the foetuses are spaced along each uterine horn. Each foetus is contained within its own membranes and has its own placenta from which it derives nourishment. At parturition, the queen will lose 40% of the weight she has gained during the pregnancy. Mammary development is palpable during the last few days of pregnancy.

I cannot stress often enough that pregnancy is not a disease but a natural occurrence; thus, in order to maximise the chances of an easy birth and good mothering skills, the owner should let the queen lead as normal a life as possible. However, there are some areas which should be carefully monitored. Firstly, she will need a different feeding regime. The unborn kittens place huge demands on the queen's own body reserves, so once the queen is known to be pregnant (certainly by week 3) the amount of food should be increased gradually until the time of the birth when she should be consuming one and a half times her normal daily intake. The queen should be fed little and often because she will be physically unable to eat large meals as her body expands with the unborn kittens. The food offered should be high in proteins and nutrients and the best feeds to give at this stage are those designed for kittens. Food intake will vary according to the size of the litter so, if the queen is hungry, give food. I always leave a bowl of kitten kibble down for the queen to graze on if she gets peckish. Cats are all individual and no food quantities should be adhered to strictly; a queen may need less if carrying only one kitten and those carrying a large litter may be ravenous. If at all possible, it is best to avoid giving medication such as antibiotics during pregnancy and flea and worm treatments should have been done prior to the cat becoming pregnant. The vaccinations should also be up to date before the queen is mated. If the pregnancy is unplanned, do not use chemicals. Throughout the pregnancy, monitor the health of the cat closely; check for vaginal discharge and at any sign of ill health, consult your vet. I would advise anyone with a pregnant cat not to allow the cat to roam freely; she will be safer if confined. The change in a queen's physical size during pregnancy can make her slower and more likely to be injured. She may also kitten outside. In the last week of pregnancy, the cat will seek a place to give birth to her kittens; if at all possible, it is best to confine her to an area where the birth will be accessible – best of British! I have the most sophisticated kittening boxes that cost a fortune and over the years, cats have shunned my purpose-built boxes for the linen basket or almost invariably, my bed, but now I have got it cracked. The kittening box is placed on my bed and the queen is quite happy to stay in the box as long as I lie next to it. It is important that she has a designated area in which to give birth and it should be somewhere quiet and private, in a draught free room at a constant temperature of 18-24c. A cardboard box will do, with comfortable bedding which should be flat as possible so the kittens cannot get tangled up in folds or wedged round the edges. I always kitten my queens on soft towelling, cut to size for the kitten box and sewn together so it is triple thickness.

Chapter 8. Parturition and Lactation

When you know that your queen will be having kittens, it is important to be prepared and have your birthing kit ready well before the due date. The cat will now be used to the designated kittening area but there are a number of items you will need to have readily to hand. Tincture of iodine can be used to disinfect the umbilical cords. A queen will sever the umbilical cord by chewing it and if possible, her mouth should be free of dental disease as this is a source of infection. Sometimes, the kittens arrive too rapidly for the queen to clean and sever the cords of each one and when this happens, the breeder must intervene and give her assistance; sterile, sharp, blunt tipped scissors are ideal for this job. You will need plenty of towels and clean flannels for grasping kittens should you need to assist delivery. Make sure you have first life drops and powdered colostrum in your store cupboard to aid any weak kittens and you may also need a powdered complete milk replacer, specifically for kittens. There are a number of different brands of this product available and in the event of any problems, you should be prepared to supplement the feeding of, and/or hand rear kittens. A cat carrier should be ready for use if an emergency trip to the vet is needed. A clock or watch to time the labour and a notepad and pen so you can record your observations are also useful.

Finally, the long awaited day arrives; you will experience mixed emotions, primarily excitement but this will be tinged with apprehension. After over thirty years of breeding, I still worry myself sick until the kittens and mum are safely delivered; the day I don't worry will be the day I give up breeding because it will mean I no longer care. When your queen is reaching her due date you must be there with her. I have lost count of the times I have cancelled outings because I have a queen due and I will not leave her. Pregnancies should be planned; if you work away from home, take your annual leave when the kittens are due and do not plan to go away until the kittens have gone to their new homes.

Parturition or labour can be divided into three stages. The first stage consists of the relaxation of the cervix and the vagina. There will be intermittent contractions of the uterus. At this stage, the queen can appear restless and may be more vocal; during this time, my own cats make it clear they want me in attendance. The contractions are slight and spaced out and often the first contractions are no more than a rippling down the spine; they then increase in intensity and the queen may extend her back leg. The contractions are followed by a period of relaxation which serves to prevent the foetal blood supply being cut off. The pelvic muscles slacken and the area between the anus and the vulva loosens. The cat will make repeated visits to the kittening box and will scratch up the bed in an attempt to make a nest in which to give birth. Some queens refuse food at this stage and others have a reduced appetite. A few days before kittening, the cat's temperature may fall below 100f and usually, it is consistently low in the last 24 hours, but not always. There may be a vaginal discharge, although this may be difficult to detect as cats are so fastidious about cleanliness. A normal first stage can last up to 36 hours, particularly with maiden queens who tend to take much longer than established queens who have kittened before.

In the second stage, the uterine contractions become stronger and more frequent and propel the foetus towards and into the pelvic opening. As the first foetus enters the pelvis, a small bag of amniotic fluid is visible at the vulva which then bursts; this is the outer layer of foetal membrane. The external fluid is usually cleaned up by the cat and the inner layer passes into the pelvis which retains some fluid to act as a lubricant. Fluid plays an important part as the pressure causes the dilation of the already relaxed cervix and vagina. In an ideal world, the fluid membranes are followed by the wedge shaped head of the foetus although many of the kittens I have delivered have been breach births (bottom first). Whilst this is not abnormal, in my experience it takes longer for these kittens to be expelled. At this point the contractions are intense; the cat will either push its back legs against the kitten box to get extra leverage or will sit up and bear down. My queens often pant at this stage; usually the panting takes place in the first stage but Somalis leave it for the second stage. Once the head is out of the vulva, one or two strains should deliver the kitten. It normally takes from five to thirty minutes from the start of the second stage to complete the delivery.

The third stage follows immediately and is simply the passage of membranes, complete with the placenta (afterbirth) which, when healthy, resembles liver. At this stage the segment of the uterus from which the kitten has come contracts back into shape and shortens. Normally, after each kitten, the placenta is passed but when two kittens are born in quick succession, both placentas can be expelled together. It is essential that all the placentas are counted – one placenta per kitten - as placental retention can cause major problems to the health of the queen. Most queens eat the placenta, an instinctive protective behaviour retained from the wild where evidence of parturition might attract predators. If the queen has a large litter, she may only eat some of the placentas and the rest should be removed. The queen should be encouraged to eat the placenta because it contains an endocrine gland which will stimulate the flow of milk to the teats. As each kitten is born, instinct will tell the queen to break open the sac with her teeth to release the kitten and she will clean its face of all mucous matter so that it can breathe. She will then rub her rough tongue all over the kitten, which not only cleans away unwanted matter but also acts as a massage, encouraging the kitten to move about and get it's lungs working. If the queen knows what she is doing, it is best not to interfere but if she is inexperienced and does not break the sac, the owner must act promptly to prevent the kitten suffocating. Once the sac has been broken, the queen will set about chewing through the umbilical cord and when the chord has been severed, then the queen will eat the placenta. Second and third stages of labour are repeated as each kitten is born. The interval between kittens can vary from a few minutes to over an hour. This is when you really need to know your cat; if the queen is relaxed and happy, panic ye not and go with the flow! She will soon tell you if things are not right and it may take well over a day for an entire litter to be born. I really cannot stress how important it is to be with the queen and to be aware of all the signs that could indicate a complicated birth; the lives of the queen and kittens depend upon the owner knowing what to do. Sometimes you can experience something known as 'interrupted labour' when the queen ceases straining. She may settle down happily with her kittens suckling and may even eat, yet it is obvious from her size and palpation that there are more kittens to be born. This resting stage can last up to 36 hours and then the rest of the kittens will be born quite naturally.

I have bred cats for over thirty years and there is no better sight than a queen curled up with a litter of kittens, all at the milk bar and safely delivered. I still sit and worry all through the labour in case something goes wrong and sometimes there is heartache, but I have lived with some wonderful cats over this time and met some fantastic people; my hobby of breeding cats has turned into a passion and a way of life.

Signs indicating all is not as it should be.
Most births present no problems but when a difficult birth (dystocia) occurs the owner needs to know when to intervene. I would seek veterinary advice if my queen was over 67 days as my mating dates are definite and matings are supervised. If the queen is in intense labour between 30-60 minutes and the kitten has not been expelled or is not visible, this could be indicative of either a disorder due to inadequate size of the birth canal, or injury. If the kitten has been visible at the vulva and ten minutes of intensive contractions have not expelled or propelled it further forward, and gentle traction on the trapped foetus causes the queen pain, the kitten may be mal-presented or malformed, too large or be dead. I have intervened when a kitten is trapped, working with the queen's contractions and gently rotating the kitten in a downward movement until it slips free but great care must be taken and this intervention should only be performed if it is clear that the kitten is stuck. Once the kitten is out, the membranes must be removed immediately from the mouth and nose to enable the kitten to breathe. The queen may become agitated, crying and coming out of the box and

repeatedly going to the tray and straining, almost similar to exaggerated symptoms of cystitis. This is indicative that a kitten is stuck. If the queen is unwell in herself, depressed, lethargic, running a fever or has an unpleasant discharge, then she must be taken to the vet. If the queen cries or bites at her vulva, or loses fresh blood from her vulva for more than ten minutes and no kittens have been born, this is not a good sign; however, do bear in mind that there is always evidence of some fresh blood in kittening. This happened to one of my own queens a few years ago and prompt attention meant she and her six kittens (born by caesarean section) all lived to tell the tale. If there are still kittens to be born after 36 hours a trip to the vet is called for. Sometimes, uterine inertia can happen although this is quite rare in the cat and usually associated with low litter numbers. In my experience, single kittens often present problems during the birth and if they survive, continue to be a problem as they have no litter mates to develop alongside. The queen is also less attentive with one kitten and soon gets bored with not enough paws to look after! For that reason I dread a singleton.

The size of litters can be affected by a number of factors. Cats who roam free will often mate with multiple males and produce kittens from different fathers in the same litter. The female is allowed to mate freely when she is at her most receptive, whereas in a controlled breeding situation there is not the optimum chance of conception, thus, as a general rule, the litter size from controlled matings will be smaller. Another factor which can affect the litter size is the age of the queen; whilst cats can continue to breed safely up to the age of ten, the number of kittens will usually decrease. I do not breed from my girls beyond eight years of age, although to prove there is nothing set in stone, my beloved Lulu had her last and biggest litter of seven kittens aged 8! I would also like to comment here that I find it disappointing that the GCCF, unlike the Kennel Club, do not recommend a set age range for breeding as queens deserve a retirement.

The length of gestation can vary and there is evidence that a large litter will have a shorter pregnancy I experienced this many years ago with a Burmese who gave birth to 13 kittens on day 60. They were all small and despite every effort on my part, only 7 survived. The exact opposite seems to be true of single kittens who appear very reluctant to make an appearance in the world, frequently going on to day 67 and being very large.

All breeders should be aware that there are some congenital diseases which affect kittens and, depending on the severity, may be fatal. Congenital disease is disease which is present at birth or which is transmitted directly from the parents.

Cleft Palate. This is a defect in the roof of the mouth, consisting of a gap in the structures forming the palate; there are varying degrees of severity but in the most severe cases this defect allows communication between the mouth and nasal passages. This means that when the kitten suckles, the milk comes down the nose. In severe cases, the kitten is unable to suck and will die soon after birth. Less severe cases can present as kittens not thriving as well as their litter mates as the nutrients they are getting are not sufficient.

Hernia. In a typical abdominal hernia there are two parts; firstly, the ring or opening in the muscular wall of the abdomen and secondly, a swelling appearing below the skin composed of the hernia sac and its contents. The contents vary according to the situation, size, and nature of the hernia. A small ringed umbilical hernia is a slight defect and can be repaired quite easily with one or two stitches; these can be caused by an over enthusiastic queen when she is chewing the chord at the time of birth. However, some kittens may be born with virtually no abdominal musculature and part of the bowel, stomach, bladder, or liver may be visible. In these cases, euthanasia is the only option. Sadly some years ago I had a Burmese kitten born with such a deformity and he was put to sleep immediately.

Spina Bifida. This is an abnormality of the vertebral column which involves a defect in the closure of the arch formed by the dorsal laminae of one or more vertebrae. Once again, there are degrees of severity; the worst lesions prove fatal and in these cases you can feel where the spine has not closed and there is a visible concavity to the spine, usually just behind the shoulders. Less severe cases can cause paralysis and incontinence.

The first hurdle is over; the queen is delivered and you have a litter of healthy kittens. Half the deaths of kittens around the time of birth or within the first few days of life are due to poor management at delivery; thus the following simple and effective procedures should be put in place by the breeder. Warmth is one of the most important factors for new born kittens. Kittens are unable to regulate their own body temperature at birth and their internal temperature is 3 degrees lower than at 5 weeks of age. They are sensitive to cold and as soon as they are chilled, their movements slow down and they are unable to suckle or absorb milk efficiently. If the kitten is not suffering from hypothermia, the mother makes an ideal hot water bottle. The temperature of the kitten box is crucial; it should be 30 degrees centigrade in the first week and then gradually lowered as the kitten grows. To raise the temperature of a struggling kitten, ensure it is thoroughly dry by rubbing it dry with towelling; do not use a direct heat source such as a hairdryer. The best way is to place the kitten next to your skin under a layer of clothing. It may take up to three hours to warm the kitten.

The other critical factor with new born kittens is humidity. Because the kitten box is heated the air dries out faster. A new born kitten is made up of 80% water and the skin dehydrates very rapidly. The humidity can be regulated by placing containers of water or a cool mist humidifier in the room. A kitten who dehydrates at birth rapidly loses weight; very often a healthy kitten will lose a small amount of weight in the first 24 hours but re-gain it later on. If the kitten loses 10% or more of its body weight, it will need warm sugary water or an oral electrolyte solution which can be administered from a feeding bottle.

Once the kittens have been born, the queen will usually be extremely attentive to their needs. Many cats will only leave their babies to eat, drink and use the tray and some will do this for up to 2 weeks. My own girls are excellent mothers but are only this attentive for a few days. There can be a change in behaviour; some become more affectionate and some more aggressive as they protect their brood. I am very fortunate that all my queens share their babies with me; sometimes too much! Some of my queens love to sleep with me and when they leave the kitten box to come to bed, naturally the kittens cry. Initially, this involves the queen running from bed to box countless times during the night, but they soon solve the problem by moving their kittens into my bed! I give in and let the kittens stay, but in their own fluffy high sided bed so they are safe. I monitor the queen closely during the first few days after kittening. It is not usual for there to be problems but you should be aware of what might go wrong. I check the queen's teats daily as she will be producing milk and her dietary requirements will alter. The queen loses 40% of her weight after kittening, so she will appear much smaller. The kittens are also checked regularly; each day, I weigh them and record their development on weight charts. If I was worried about a kitten, I would monitor it's weight twice daily. The queen's hormone levels will alter and if you are unlucky, she may come in to call again in the first six weeks. This can be a problem because the milk levels will drop and she will not be as attentive to her kittens.

The breeder must monitor the queen very closely for the first few days after kittening to make sure there are no problems developing. Blood loss after kittening is minimal but there are cases when the queen continues to bleed and this needs veterinary attention. If the queen is restless in the first few days, has a poor appetite and has a brownish vaginal discharge, this could be indicative that a placenta has been retained and again, veterinary help is essential. The uterus can become infected which usually manifests itself during the first 3 days by the queen becoming lethargic, ignoring her kittens, refusing food, vomiting and having a fever. When the abdomen is palpated she may be in pain and veterinary help is needed. Rarely, a cat may continue to strain after the birth of the kittens and this is due to a uterine prolapse; when this occurs, the prolapsed uterus can be seen clearly at the vulva and this constitutes an emergency.

The queen needs constant monitoring; the nipples should be checked daily because they can become infected; this type of infection is called mastitis.

It usually affects only one gland and may be due to too much milk, or the kittens not suckling from that particular teat. It will be hot, painful and enlarged. By using mild heat and massage, the milk can be released but if there is an abscess present, the queen will be dull and feverish, a purplish area around the teat will appear and it can rupture. Another condition owners should be aware of is eclampsia which usually happens later, from 17 days to 8 weeks. The first signs are hypersensitivity to stimuli, twitching and a staggering gait which, if ignored, can lead to coma and death. Eclampsia is caused by a sudden drop in calcium levels and an intravenous injection of calcium solution can produce miraculous results.

In order to maintain the health of the queen, the most important input from the owner is the correct diet. A lactating queen has to feed not only herself but also her kittens; the strain on her body is immense. By the time the kittens are 4 weeks old, the queen needs 3 times their normal intake of food. It is advisable to feed a high quality food ad lib and kitten food is best as it contains moderate levels of calcium. It is inevitable, however careful you are, that there will be some weight loss during the six weeks and some queens lose more weight than others.

Throughout the early weeks, whilst the mother and kittens are using the kitten box, it should be kept scrupulously clean. I do not change the birth bedding straight away; if the kittens are born at night, I change it in the morning and vice versa as the scent of the birthing bed settles the queen. I use absorbent bedding with a heated pad underneath so the kittens will not get cold. I then change the bedding (daily as a rule) but if it is soiled then it is changed as required. Cats have a habit of moving their kittens around; if they are happy with their surroundings, they will stay put.

If the queen comes in to call in the first few weeks after giving birth, then it is important she is confined to barracks - the last thing you need is for her to get pregnant again or, even worse, be injured as she wanders off looking for a mate. I think it totally irresponsible to let a nursing queen roam free.

If the queen becomes more affectionate, then interact with her. If she is aggressive, give her privacy but however aggressive she may be, her health and that of the kittens must be monitored, but with minimal interference. Usually, if a queen behaves aggressively when she has kittens, it is only for a short while as it should be uncharacteristic. If the cat has a tendency towards aggressive behaviour ordinarily, then that cat should not have been bred from!

With the birth of your kittens complete and a healthy mum and babies, you can relax and enjoy the next three months as the kittens grow and develop.

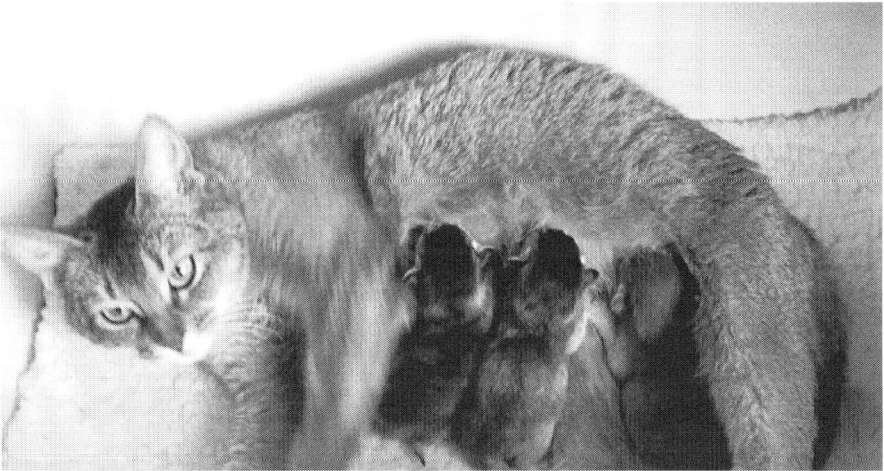

Chapter 9. Rearing Your Kittens

There may be some occasions when it will be necessary to hand rear kittens; this could be due to the fact that the queen is unable to care for them or the litter is too large for her to rear unaided.

I would like to make some general comments about hand rearing kittens to begin with. I have hand reared kittens successfully over the years but it is not a task to be taken on lightly. It requires immense dedication and commitment. It is a 24/7 job and if the owner cannot be available all day and all night, it is totally impractical to try it. There can be behavioural problems in cats which are hand reared and trying to replace the natural nutrition of the mother's milk is very difficult. For this reason, I only do it as a last resort; when possible, I use a foster mother but if there is not one available, I feed the kittens myself and then have a queen to help in all the other areas. I am very fortunate that I have retired queens who no longer produce milk but will clean the kittens and teach them how to be cats; they can do this much better than me. Fortunately, the Somali is a generous spirited breed and the queens, even when retired, never lose their maternal instincts and happily play the role of aunty.

A new born kitten needs 10 feeds a day and strict feeding times must be adhered to; when the kitten gets hungry, it will move about in search of milk, soon tire and fall asleep which is not beneficial. The kitten should be kept in a warm environment; kittens cannot control their body temperature and one of the major problems of hand rearing is the onset of hypothermia, so the box should have a maintained temperature of 85-90f but should be large enough for the kitten to crawl away from the heat source if it is too warm. I use heated pads at the base of the box. As the kittens get older, the temperature can be reduced gradually and 72f is perfectly acceptable by the end of the first month. A room temperature of 75f is adequate. If all is well, whilst asleep the kitten's bodies should be relaxed and warm and twitching gently. To ensure that the temperature is correct, a thermometer should be placed in the box.

Kittens are very fragile and can become ill and die very quickly; hand reared kittens can easily become dehydrated and starve, so the feeding regime is vital. If kittens are hand reared from the moment they are born, they are missing a crucial element; their first drink of mother's milk. The first milk contains colostrum which has a large amount of milk proteins and is vital for the kitten. Fortunately, there is now a product called Collate which I swear by and there is also available a tub of First Life kitten colostrum, a powder which is mixed with water. Another product I find invaluable is First Life kitten drops. I give all my kittens 3 drops of this whether they have problems or not and also give it to the queen once she has kittened. There are numerous brands of replacement milk on the market now; when I first started breeding there was no choice - it was Lactol or nothing. Whichever product you use, the directions are clear as to how to mix it and what quantities should be given at each stage. As the kittens grow older, the number of feeds can be reduced and the time interval extended; by the time the kittens are 2 weeks old, you might be able to get 6 hours uninterrupted sleep. By then, you will need it!

There are various ways of feeding kittens and you can buy baby bottles specifically designed for them. However, the size of the hole in the teat is critical; too small, and the kitten won't get any milk and too large, the kitten will choke. You can spoon feed, but this requires practice and it can be dangerous as the lungs can fill with milk - I have never used this method. You can use a dropper, which is similar but quicker and cleaner. A syringe can be used but there is always the danger that if the plunger sticks and then gives way suddenly, the excess milk may fill the lungs and cause drowning. Tube feeding can be done but requires skill and knowledge; whilst it is clean and efficient, it is not without its drawbacks as there is no control over how much is fed and too much or too little can be given. The kitten is also deprived of sucking and those with a strong sucking reflex may suck on each other which may result in skin problems, and often psychological damage may develop later in life. My favourite method, developed over the years, is a combination of dropper and bottle. I use a dropper, but with a tapered end that the kitten can wrap its tongue round and suck; it is safe, the kitten doesn't run the risk of drowning and I know exactly how much the has been ingested as the dropper is marked in mls. All feeding equipment should be kept clean; good hygiene is paramount when rearing kittens as they are prone to infections. Utensils used for preparing milk should be sterile. The kitten's weight must be monitored by weighing them daily.

Having fed the kitten, it is now time to pay attention to the other end! Kittens under 2 weeks of age have to be stimulated to urinate and defecate. The kitten has a voiding reflex which the mother stimulates by licking the anus and genital areas. If the mother is not available, the carer must simulate this action. This needs to be done for up to 4 weeks or until the kitten is independent. I use cotton wool and stimulate before and after feeding and from 3 weeks of age, the kitten can be placed on the litter tray as this should trigger the reflex. Constipation is a common problem with hand reared kittens and so is diarrhoea; therefore the kitten's motions must be monitored closely.

Well, what more can I say? By the time you have hand reared your kittens, your sleep pattern is ruined and you are a nervous wreck because you are monitoring the kittens night and day, very aware that should they become ill, time is of the essence as a sick kitten can die very quickly. At four weeks, you can start to breathe a sigh of relief and realise what a rewarding experience you have had.

The vast majority of litters are born with no complications and the mother rears the kittens herself; nothing is more fascinating than observing how these little creatures develop over the first few weeks of their lives. Generally, for the first 2 weeks, all a kitten does is eat and sleep. They are deaf and blind. From the moment they are born, they can crawl to the teat. Their eyes are closed and as a general rule they do not open until around 7 - 10 days of age. During this period, their hearing will also develop. There will always be exceptions and there have been cases of kittens born with their eyes open, but this is usually indicative of a health problem. With the senses improving, the kitten will begin to explore the kitten box and show signs of play behaviour. At first, the kittens will pat each other in a clumsy fashion, but as their sight and hearing improves, they will watch their mother come and go from the kitten box. Kittens, from the moment of birth, although helpless, can spit when picked up until they are familiar with the voice and smell of the human. By 3 weeks of age, the kittens can toddle a short distance on wobbly legs - I love this stage, it is so endearing. They are also capable of rolling over and righting themselves, and playing with their siblings. By the end of the fourth week the kitten is up and running, exploring outside the kitten box and only returning to the box if frightened or for a cuddle with mum. The kittens start to eat solids at this age. When I first started breeding, I read numerous books which told me how to wean kittens; in my opinion, it is totally unnecessary – the kitten knows best. They will eat solids when they are good and ready and in a litter there can be a variance of a few days. As long as appropriate food is available, they will eventually climb into the dish! Their table manners are messy to begin with and will often stand in the dish to eat the surrounding food, but it takes very little training to teach them to eat nicely! Care must be taken at this age because they will lick and chew things to test the surfaces. No wires should be accessible and great care should be taken with cleaning products. Up to this point, the kittens should have been handled regularly, although not too much at birth as the bond between mother and kittens should not be interfered with. Fortunately, my girls share their kittens with me quite happily although I have noticed over the years a reticence from queens I have bought in who were not home bred; hence the following is most important. Handling from 2-8 weeks is essential. In the wild, this is the period when the nest would be changed and kittens start to recognise danger and safety. Gentle grooming should begin now and the ears and mouth should be checked, thus making health monitoring easy for the future. Training done in these weeks lasts for a lifetime. At five weeks the brain is almost mature, but the motor skills are still not fully developed so it is important to protect the kittens from possible injury at this stage. They need space and need to play; toys should be available such as ping pong balls, feathers, boxes and paper bags. Food offered can be varied so that they do not become conservative in their tastes in later life; there are many kitten diets on the market. At this stage, they should be placed on a litter tray after eating. Again, I am very fortunate as it is rare that I have to litter train a kitten; the mother deposits them in the tray herself and stands guard until they have performed! During this time the kitten should be introduced to new people, children, dogs and household noises such as washing machines, vacuums, televisions etc. I cannot stress how important it is to socialise kittens; if they do not receive the proper stimuli at this stage, they could become difficult to handle in later life. Sadly, I have seen this far too often in the boarding cattery I run and it is an experience shared with many vets; whilst the difficult cat is OK in its home environment, it cannot cope when removed from that environment.

Play is very important in the development of the kitten and the mother's role is paramount. At a young age she will entice her offspring to play, usually with the end of her tail; she also teaches them to be independent at about 8 weeks by refusing to allow them to continue to suckle.

From 4-8 weeks of age, kittens will develop the following skills used in play. They arch their backs and turn sideways on to give the impression of a larger image and they approach each other with side-ways steps – I just love that sight! At 5 weeks, they will learn to pounce and soon afterwards they will stand on their hind legs and box the air with their paws. At 6 weeks they will begin chasing each other and soon they will be able to leap right up into the air to avoid each other during chasing games. From 7 weeks onwards, they will play hide and seek and lie in wait before pouncing and chasing. From 8 weeks on, the play becomes more sophisticated and the hunting and killing actions are apparent in the play. They are so expert at dribbling small balls, I sometimes think my kittens would do a better job than the English football team! They learn to carry small toys in their mouths and may growl if another kitten approaches. Play within the litter at this stage can appear to be quite aggressive; the kittens practice using their forepaws to grasp whilst they bite the necks of their litter mates. The hind legs are used for raking at the body of another kitten whilst the forepaws grasp it firmly round the neck.

At about 12 weeks the kitten is independent enough to go to its new home. My kittens leave me after 13 weeks when fully vaccinated. In all the years I have been breeding, there is no sight I love better than a mother safely delivered with her wet new born kittens suckling from her. People ask me how can I part with them but I always view my kittens as babies that I am looking after for someone else. I have all the pleasure of those first few months and it is my responsibility to the cat and his future owner to bring up a happy, well balanced kitten who will become a valued, well-adjusted member of a new family for at least 15 years. Once the litter of kittens have gone to their new homes, there will be a huge gap in your life and household. The whole process may have been hard work and a shock to the system but there is only one way to fill the void you are left with – yes – you've guessed it - start preparing for another visit in a few months' time to the stud.

Chapter 10. Preventive Healthcare

Hundreds of books have been written on veterinary matters relating to cats but I feel that I should address some areas of feline health, particularly that of preventative medicine.

Before I outline preventative healthcare, I would like to make a general comment which applies to ALL ages. The cat is a predator and so adept at hiding illness and pain, therefore it is essential that there are regular health checks; I would advise twice yearly checks, even if there is no apparent problem. As a cattery owner, I see cats at intervals and often spot potential problems to which I can alert the owner. They have been oblivious of the problem and in many cases this has prolonged the life of the cat. I know we are in an economic downturn but regular check- ups can not only prolong quality of life but save money in the long term. I always advise the owners of my kittens to take out pet insurance because when major problems arise, the vet bills can be astronomical.

Vaccination. At the moment, this subject is a 'hot potato' and there are many diverse views. In a boarding cattery, the requirement is that all cats should have a current vaccination i.e. done within the last twelve months. I also show my cats and the GCCF insist that all vaccinations should be current; failure to present valid evidence of vaccination means that the cat will be rejected at vetting in. A few years ago there was evidence, particularly associated with the FeLV vaccine, that a sarcoma could develop at the vaccine site. This was initially found in the USA but subsequently, cases were being seen in the UK. On the advice of the late Miss Julia May, I started to request the FeLV vaccine was done in the leg as it is easier to remove a tumour from the leg, by amputation if necessary, rather than from the neck area. Everyone knows that there can be reactions to vaccines; some may be minor but inevitably they cause concern. Some years ago, there were fears about human vaccines in babies and a lot of worried parents opted out of the measles vaccine; the result has been a resurgence of the disease. Therefore, at present I support and encourage regular vaccination but the situation should continue to be monitored and manufacturer's guide lines followed. There are times when a cat may be ill or on certain medication when vaccination is not an option. Also, the life style of the cat should be considered; if it is an only cat, kept solely indoors, it has a low risk of infection by FeLV or Chlamydophila. Owners should be made aware that not all vaccines give the same level of protection. Vaccines for feline panleucopenia are very effective (Feline Parvo virus), whereas vaccines for Feline Calici virus, herpes virus and Clamydia (although protecting the cat and reducing the severity of the disease) do not totally prevent the cat contracting the disease. Also, the cat can become a carrier and thus pass the disease on to others.

The first vaccination administered to kittens is slightly different as it consists of 2 injections given 3 and no more than 4 weeks apart and then annually thereafter.

Worming. I always worm my queens before they are mated. My kittens are wormed at six weeks onwards. There are different types of worms and different preparations. Worming treatment comes in liquid, granular and tablet form. Kittens should be treated against roundworm (from 6 -16 weeks of age) and this is important because round worms can be transmitted to humans (zoonosis).

Adult cats should be treated every 2-3 months if they are outdoor cats who hunt freely. Indoor cats may go as long as 6 months; however, all my cats who live inside are wormed every 3 months. Adult cats should be treated for round worm and tapeworm. The presence of intestinal parasites is detrimental to the health of the cat. Kittens who have worms will not thrive and can be subject to bouts of diarrhoea. Tapeworm can also be transmitted to humans; sometimes there are no clinical symptoms of infection in the cat but tapeworms can cause anaemia, and in severe cases, blockage of the intestine. However, there are visible signs of tapeworm in the presence of mature segments on faeces or on the hair around the anus, which when they dry out resemble grains of rice. The cystic stage can also affect the brain. Cats may become infected through swallowing a flea.

Flea Treatment. Flea treatment is very important because fleas have a detrimental effect on the health of the cat. The cat flea (Ctenocephalides felis) is the major culprit but cats can be infested with hedgehog fleas and rabbit fleas and with tape worms if it eats a flea whilst grooming. Adult fleas live on the blood of the host and a heavy infestation in kittens can cause weakness, anaemia and death. Fleas may carry infectious diseases such as FIA (feline infectious anaemia). Fleas can also cause allergic reactions in cats, making them scratch, bite and lick excessively, causing hair loss leading to miliary dermatitis. Cat fleas can also bite humans and result in itching in sensitive humans.

There is a vast array of products on the market for the treatment of fleas. Some are more effective than others. Cheap powders and flea collars can be bought over the counter but they are not very effective. Powders are only active whilst they remain on the coat and a cat will naturally lick the offending compound off the coat which can cause breathing difficulties and is of no benefit to the cat. Flea collars treat the neck area instead of the whole coat and often there is a fur loss at the site of the collar. They also have no quick release catch and are a hazard if the cat gets snagged whilst out hunting.

Some products come in pump action sprays but cats do not like the noise these make; the coat must be sprayed so it is wet all over and again the cat will instinctively try to lick the product to remove it from the coat.

There are a number of spot on treatments; these are drops which are applied to the skin at the back of the neck behind the skull and between the shoulder blades. The product is then distributed throughout the rest of the body. They are easy to administer and the cat finds the area hard to groom. I always use this at night time when my cats will sleep. Spot on treatments vary as to what they target; some kill adult fleas and these are best used on cats which are sensitive to the flea bite. Others interrupt the development of the flea by preventing growth and reproduction. Some also can be used to eradicate ticks and others have worming treatment included.

Flea products contain various chemicals which include organophosphate, carbamate, pyrethroid, or pyrethrum. Those that interfere with the development of the flea may contain fipronil, imidacloprid, or selamectin.

To be effective, the manufacturer's guidelines should be followed as to the frequency of use. NEVER use out of date products and NEVER use dog flea treatments on cats as this could be fatal; it has happened in the past.

Dental Checks. Oh dear - this is one area of feline health that is the bug bear of my life! In the early days, Somalis were very prone to gingivitis and stomatitis; fortunately, through selective breeding, we have reduced the problem but I still take extreme care where my cats mouths are concerned. All my kittens are very used to having their mouths opened and their teeth checked before they leave me. Their new owners are given instructions about using dental diets e.g. Hills TD, and shown how to brush their teeth. I find that a little rubber cap attachment to the finger with an oral paste is least stressful for my cats but brushes can also be used. It is very important to check for dental disease as it has an impact on the health and quality of life of the cat. Kittens need to be checked to make sure their permanent teeth are erupting correctly and their teeth should be monitored throughout their life. With the ageing cat, particular attention should be paid to apparent decreased quality of life and inability to eat which may be due to dental disease or tumours.

There are a number of common oral diseases.

Periodontitis (gum disease). This is caused by plaque which, if left to build up, will lead to gingivitis which in turn will result in inflammation and loss of the supporting structures of the tooth.

Feline Resorption Lesions (neck lesions). The exact cause is not known but this is a complex disease with several causal factors. There are two types; one where lesions are confined to the cement-enamel junction and the other which involves the root. The two types are indistinguishable and x-rays need to be taken to ascertain which it is and then the appropriate treatment may be determined.

Chronic Gingivostomatitis. Again, this is very complex and it is thought to be an immune response to plaque. It is very difficult to treat and may result in extractions to reduce the presence of bacteria in the mouth.

Fractured Teeth. If the pulp cavity is exposed, this can lead to infection and inflammation around the tooth so treatment will be required.

A dental check-up can also monitor the condition of the tongue and detect the presence of oral tumours

Regular health check-ups. These are most important and twice yearly check ups are advisable. There are a number of reasons for this. Firstly, it is the ideal way to get to know your vet and for the vet to get to know your cat. In my boarding cattery, I see my feline guests at intervals throughout the year. Often I can spot something that the owner is unaware of because I notice a change in the cat, either physically or behaviourally. The vet who sees a cat twice yearly has the same opportunity. The vet can monitor the general health, check the heart, eyes, ears (for the presence of ear mites), mouth, weight and mobility. It is an opportunity for the vet to ask the owner pertinent questions regarding increased sleeping or decreased activity. The vet can educate the owner in the subtle behavioural changes that are not just age related. It is very important to monitor the weight of older cats; the onset of obesity can be seen in a cat in their prime and, just like human beings, weight is easy to put on but difficult to lose!

Chapter 11. Infectious Diseases

There are numerous conditions which can affect all cats and it would be remiss of me not to mention some of the major infectious conditions; the following is a brief guide to symptoms, and how the disease is transmitted. There are many veterinary hand books designed for breeders and I would advise you to have at least one detailed text book to which you can refer.

Feline Immunodeficiency Virus (FIV). This virus suppresses the immune system and thus, because secondary infections occur, it can present a number of clinical signs. During the first three months of the disease, there may be fever, general malaise and enlarged lymph nodes but often these signs go unnoticed. The clinical signs that are a direct result of the virus include blood abnormalities, inflammation of the eye and neurological disease and tumours. Secondary infections associated with FIV include gum and mouth problems e.g. gingivitis, respiratory tract infections, anaemia, skin infections, and meningitis. The cat may present with anorexia, weight loss and general lethargy.

Feline Leukaemia Virus (FeLV). This virus usually affects young cats who normally succumb to a FeLV associated disease between 3 to 5 years after being infected. The virus is similar to FIV in that sufferers can present with a number of clinical signs and diseases. Many will develop cancer of the lymph nodes and there may be difficulty in breathing, a persistent cough or vomiting. Anaemia is also commonly associated with FeLV. As with FIV, there can be non-specific symptoms such as weight loss, anorexia and fever. FeLV may also suppress the immune system, as seen with FIV.

Feline Calici Virus (FCV). Symptoms will vary with the progression of the illness but in the early stage, the main symptom will be sneezing. In later stages, there may be nasal and ocular discharge and in acute cases there will be a raised temperature, anorexia, ulceration of the tongue or median nasal septum, paw lesions, drooling saliva and pneumonic symptoms. In hyper-acute cases, there can be a massive influx of fluid to the chest which can cause sudden death.

Feline Parvovirus (FPV). This is a highly contagious infection causing severe acute diarrhoea and vomiting which leads to dehydration, reduction of white blood cells and often results in death. Fortunately, vaccination provides good protection although the mortality rate in infected young unvaccinated kittens is very high. FPV is also known as feline infectious enteritis (FIE). The virus can be transmitted by 3 routes; firstly, directly by the faecal-oral route and secondly, indirectly, which is most common. The virus can be carried on contaminated objects such as feed bowls, bedding, grooming equipment, clothing and the owner themselves. Dogs that are shedding the parvovirus can also infect cats. Thirdly, the virus can cross the placenta, causing the queen to infect her unborn kittens.

Feline Infectious Peritonitis (FIP). This is an infection in cats caused by a virulent strain of feline coronavirus (FCoV). It is a very complicated disease and is greatly feared by breeders as it can emerge with little or no warning. An entire book could be written about this disease alone and research into it is still ongoing. There is no cure and at present no suitable vaccine. The clinical signs of FIP are diverse; broadly, two forms of the disease are recognised. The first is the wet form in which fluid builds up in body cavities such as the abdomen or chest. In the second, dry form, the clinical signs are complex, including neurological disease, ocular disease, liver disease, kidney disease and intestinal disease. The course of the disease can vary from a few days to a few months. The virus is shed by the faecal-oral route. Faeces are the main source of infection and therefore the litter trays are the principle source of oral infection in a group of cats. Evidence of the virus has been found in saliva and urine but these vectors are thought to play only a minor part in the transmission of the disease from sharing feeding bowls. Trans-placental transmission has occurred but this is uncommon.

Feline Bordetellosis. This is well known in dogs as Kennel Cough and can be transmitted from dog to cat. The clinical signs are sneezing, eye and nasal discharge and cough.

Chlamydophilia Felis. In most cases, the main symptoms affect the eyes and cause conjunctivitis and enlargement of the blood vessels in the eye. There can be ocular discharge and swelling of the conjunctival tissue. Sometimes there may be a mild fever and sneezing. Chlamydia often presents initially with a watery eye which then develops into a thicker yellow discharge.

Campylobacter. This is a bacterial enteritis, the main symptoms of which are vomiting, diarrhoea, fever and lethargy.

Dermatophytosis (Ringworm). This is the most common fungal skin infection of the cat. Ringworm in the cat does not have one specific appearance; hence it is essential when making a diagnosis that a culture is grown. The most common signs are patches of hair loss with fine scaling on the skin; the lesions are rarely itchy. There can be infection of the claws and some cats will have scabbing as well as hair loss.

Feline Infectious Anaemia. This is caused by a blood parasite (haemobartonella felis) and sometimes the infection can be mild and attract no attention. In other cases, there may be listlessness and anorexia, mucous membranes will be pallid in colour and jaundice will occur in severe cases.

Toxoplasma Gondii. This is the parasite which causes toxoplasmosis, a disease of most warm blooded animals. The infection is often subclinical; however, acute toxoplasmosis can be fatal and the symptoms are fever, lethargy and loss of appetite. Chronic toxoplasmosis can be a relapsing disease leading to anaemia, nervous symptoms and there may be evidence of heart and liver disease.

Tritrichomonas Foetus. T. Foetus is a parasite which mainly causes colitis. This leads to increased defecation and the faeces range from semi-formed to liquid, with fresh blood and mucus sometimes present. The anus can become inflamed and painful and lead to rectal prolapse. This parasite usually affects young cats, with the majority being under a year old. Apart from the diarrhoea (which can be persistent, severe and foul smelling) most cats are otherwise clinically well.

There are three ways in which the risk of contracting infectious disease can be reduced.

1. Limit Overcrowding. The more cats there are in the household, the higher the risk of infectious disease. It is best to keep cats in smaller groups.

2. Use of Disinfectants. Many of the infectious diseases can be eliminated by using bleach regularly and there are specific disinfectants which target individual diseases. Care should be taken when choosing disinfectants; the phenol group should never be used as this causes toxic side effects in cats. A simple guide to ensure the disinfectant is not phenol based is to add it to water; should the solution become milky, do not use. ALWAYS read the label! I use Animal Safe and bleach but I change my disinfectants every 3 months so that infectious organisms cannot build up resistance. Other products used are Trigene and Virkon. Bowls and litter trays should be disinfected daily; I keep 2 sets of everything. Always soak, rinse and dry and use alternate sets of bowls and trays so there is no danger of any residual infection.

3. Stress. Keep stress levels to a minimum as stressful situations such as introducing a new cat, travelling, cat shows, and pregnancy can predispose the cat to develop an infectious disease.

If a cat is unwell, it will often refuse to eat which can cause major problems and inhibit recovery. If cats do not eat for a few days, they can develop a condition called hepatic lipidosis (fat accumulation in the liver) and should this occur, it will lead to liver failure. When the body is deprived of the nutrients it requires and has to break down its own reserves to provide adequate energy for everyday existence, the healing process will be delayed. This break down of reserves will lower the immune system, increase the risk of secondary infection and also lead to muscle weakness.

This may impair the efficacy of any medication being employed. The owner must encourage the cat to eat; and the following information is designed to enhance the appetite.

Odour is very important to cats; if food does not smell appealing, they will not eat it. Choose foods with a strong aroma (over the years I have found that Sardines pass the odour test) - warming food helps to enhance aroma. Remove the food regularly as the odour will diminish the longer food remains in the bowl. It is a standing joke in my house that when a tin of red salmon is opened, the family say 'You must have a sick cat'!

Offer a variety of flavours and textures; this can be done by using different varieties of food and dry and wet foods. The food can be mashed if that makes it more palatable for the cat. I have liquidised all types of food to encourage a sick cat to eat. It is best to offer no more than 2 varying types of feed at any one time. Meals should be small in size; if a human is unwell and has a poor appetite, the last thing they want is a plate piled high and the same applies to cats. It may be that the sick cat will need a specialised veterinary diet and if this is the case, it is best to introduce the diet gradually by mixing it with food that the cat knows and likes (if this is advised by the vet). Foods with a high fat content are more palatable and are most useful for cats recovering from illness.

Placement of food dishes is very important; do not place food dishes near litter trays or near water bowls. Use wide shallow bowls so the cat's whiskers do not touch the side as some cats find this disconcerting. Put the food where the cat will feel secure and safe and this will help the cat relax.

Tempt the cat by hand feeding and interaction. Some years ago, I had a cat who was extremely ill; I fed him by hand and sat with him all the time while food was being offered, talking to him and stroking him. I used to smear a small quantity of food round his lips which he licked off; food can also be smeared on the paws. Do not be tempted to force feed the cat as a) it can be dangerous if you don't know what you are doing and b) the cat will associate that food with an unpleasant experience and probably refuse to eat it in the future.

Chapter 12. Care of the Elderly Cat

Nowadays, humans are living longer and so too are cats. This is due to a number of reasons but mainly that the diet given to cats is now refined and that veterinary science has progressed over the years. Somalis who are properly cared for should expect to reach an age well into their teens. Elderly cats, even when they appear healthy, need to be monitored closely as their immune systems are not as efficient as those of the younger cat and thus they are susceptible to disease. Older cats tolerate change much less than younger animals and may be irritable when removed from their familiar surroundings. They require small feeds and often revert back to the kitten routine of 4 meals daily. They tend to be less active and sleep more so they must be kept warm and have easy access to their beds and litter tray. With the onset of old age, they are not as agile and may have stiffening of the joints. Elderly cats should be weighed regularly and observed for any changes in their behaviour or health status as prompt treatment can manage many problems associated with old age, extending not only the length of life but also improving the quality. Old age can be accompanied by a number of conditions which are usually age related. Below, I have noted some of the conditions more commonly seen in the elderly cat.

With the advances in veterinary science, HYPERTENSION is now commonly recognised in older cats. A few years ago, one of my elderly studs was diagnosed with high blood pressure and given the medication Fortekor which enabled him to lead a full and active life for many years. Blood pressure should be monitored twice yearly in the older cat, and also for cats who have any condition associated with hypertension e.g. renal disease, heart disease, hyperthyroidism and blindness.

Another condition often found in cats of advancing years is DIABETES MELLITUS. Diabetic cats need special care and careful monitoring even if they are stable. Intake of water should be carefully assessed: if it increases or fluctuates greatly from day to day, veterinary advice should be sought as this could be indicative of poor control of the disease. Food intake should be also monitored as cats need to eat before administration of insulin. Should a cat vomit after eating, the dosage levels must be discussed with the vet. The demeanour of the cat is indicative of potential problems; it should be bright and interactive and if it appears lethargic, is unsteady on its legs or licking its lips, these are signs of a possible insulin overdose. In severe cases, cats can suffer convulsions and fall into a coma. When this happens, the blood sugar levels will have dropped which is dangerous; the cat should be given glucose solution immediately or, failing that, honey should be rubbed around the gums and the cat taken to the vet as an emergency. The likelihood of an overdose is not impossible, even though the drug may have been administered correctly. Diabetic cats are prone to complications so if the cat presents with vomiting, diarrhoea, panting, loss of appetite, dehydration or even worse, total collapse, this could be indicative of ketoacidosis which can be fatal and emergency treatment is required. It is essential to maintain a strict feeding regime with regard to amounts fed and timing; insulin should also be administered at the same time daily.

Elderly cats may well suffer from ARTHRITIS which is simply the inflammation of the joints, resulting in stiffness and pain. The underlying cause can vary; it may be trauma e.g. road traffic accident, or generalised joint disease or simply old age. Usually, the cat will be on medication, such as Metacam, but these drugs do have side effects which may cause vomiting and diarrhoea. If blood is seen in either vomit or faeces, veterinary treatment should be sought and the use of the drug withdrawn until the vet has advised a course of action. The arthritic cat will have difficulty in climbing and jumping. A comfy warm bed should be at floor level and the litter tray should be easily accessible. At night, it is good practice to add extra warmth to the bed; a bag filled with a special corn which can be heated in the microwave before placing in the bed can be of great help. The advantage of this is that it supplies extra warmth and as the bag is not rigid like a hot water bottle, it envelops the body adding extra warmth to the stiff joints. Arthritic cats often struggle to clean themselves properly so they may need extra grooming.

Ageing cats can suffer from KIDNEY DISEASE; chronic renal failure in elderly cats is very common and it is likened to heart disease in man as being one of the biggest killers of cats. It is a progressive, incurable disease. It can be managed by drug and diet therapy, thus enabling the cat to gain more time and quality of life. Apart from the administration of drugs and the specialised diet, once again the cat must be carefully monitored. The cat must have access to water at all times and the amount of fluid consumed daily must be recorded; the cat must be encouraged to drink and fluid intake can be increased by adding water to the wet feed. Cats with renal problems can become dehydrated which is a major problem requiring immediate veterinary attention. The amount of urine in the tray should also be noted as in some cases the tray can be flooded with urine which again could lead to dehydration. A careful eye must be kept on general health as any sign of vomiting or diarrhoea requires veterinary treatment. Changes in behaviour such as reluctance to eat or lethargy should be noted. The cat should be weighed regularly as weight loss is a common in cats suffering from renal failure, due to their poor appetites. Regular grooming is important as these cats suffer from dull, dandruffy coats and the fur can form clumps. Like all cats, they should be kept warm and comfortable and this is particularly important because invariably, their poor body mass necessitates extra warmth.

Another common condition seen in elderly cats is HYPERTHYROIDISM, a term which describes cats who produce excessive thyroid hormones in their thyroid gland. This condition is usually seen in middle aged and elderly cats and is another progressive disease causing cats to become thin. Their coats can be in poor condition and they can be hyperactive or irritable. A cat with this condition is similar in appearance to one with renal failure and a number of actions are relevant to both illnesses when caring for the cat e.g. close monitoring, grooming and extra warmth. The cat will be on medication and the dosage will differ depending on the cat and the severity of the disease but as many as 3 doses daily may need to be given. Often these cats have other medical needs such as a heart conditions which will entail more medication. Cats with hyperthyroidism have a voracious appetite and will need more frequent feeding. A plentiful supply of water is necessary as they suffer from increased thirst and food and water intake and output must be monitored. The drugs can cause side effects so careful attention should be paid to the skin; the liver may also be affected so any signs of jaundice should be checked on a daily basis. If the cat appears unwell, the vet should be consulted.

With old age, body parts begin to wear out; the heart is particularly susceptible to wear. There are a number of heart conditions that can present problems. Firstly, there are those which the cat has been born with – congenital defects such as faulty valves and hole in the heart. Then there is heart disease which develops during the cat's life which is often secondary to other conditions such as hyperthyroidism. Cats can suffer a heart attack, a thrombosis which can lead to paralysis or high blood pressure which can lead to a cranial bleed. For this reason, careful note must be taken of the breathing, particularly if it is laboured or the cat is panting. The respiratory rate should be checked as often as possible. Mobility needs to be watched as any stiffness or lameness may be a precursor to a thrombosis. Indicators of high blood pressure include problems with vision, apparent confusion or obvious blindness. Cats may be on medication and this must be administered. Lethargy or loss of appetite should be investigated by the vet, although cats with heart conditions can typically sleep a lot. A careful eye should be kept on the membranes of the mouth and eyes; if trouble is suspected, these should be checked for any blue tinge indicating hypoxia, which is an emergency situation. Cats with heart problems need to be relaxed and stress needs to be avoided as much as possible.

As the cat advances in years, there will inevitably be some changes in his lifestyle. Exercise will diminish and because of lack of wear, the claws will need trimming. Bladder control may weaken and therefore it is best to have litter trays easily accessible in more than one room. The cat will require more warmth and will sleep for longer periods. Elderly cats do not like change and this can present the owner with problems.

There is one area of cat care that I have not discussed as yet and should be mentioned. When owners go on holiday, provision must be made for care of their cat. There are a number of options. Firstly, a neighbour can pop in and feed the cat although personally, I never feel this is adequate; the cat will have little company (which certainly won't suit a Somali) and it is not monitored sufficiently. In the case of elderly cats on medication, this is not a realistic option. Secondly, there are Pet Sitters who will come and live in your home with your cat whilst you are away. The advantage of this is that the cat has 24/7 care and is not stressed by moving from its own environment. The disadvantage is that some people are reluctant to let strangers have the run of their house in their absence. Thirdly, there are boarding catteries and although I own one, I am well aware there are some boarding catteries that are well below the standard that is acceptable.

When choosing a cattery, the following points should be assessed.

The cattery should be clean with no overpowering smell of urine. It should be tidy and well organised. Proof of vaccination should be requested. Each cat should have its own unit and share only if there is another cat from the same household. The units should be separated by either at least a two foot space or sneeze barriers, so no cat can come into contact with another. The units should be heated and spacious. The cats should have plenty of stimuli so they don't get bored. Look at the cats in the cattery; if they are happy and relaxed then you should have no worries. Meet the staff; they should be interested to learn all about your cat. Be prepared for the cattery to ask you questions; the more they know about your cat, the easier it will be for it to settle in to its new surroundings. The most important advice I can give anyone is to make a habit of boarding your cat on a regular basis whilst it is young. This will pay dividends when the cat becomes elderly as it will be well used to the cattery, so reducing the element of stress. Also, the staff will know your cat and will spot any slight change in their behaviour. For more detailed information about how to choose a boarding cattery, contact the FAB or visit their website.

It is impossible to write about the care of the elderly cat without discussing euthanasia. The only problem with all our pets is that they do not live long enough. In an ideal world, it would be lovely if our cats lived to about twenty and died in their sleep, but that rarely happens. At some point the owner has to make a decision about putting the cat to sleep. Let me state now that you will always have a guilt trip – 'did you do it too soon or was it too late?' That is human nature. When the cat no longer has a quality of life, then however difficult it is, we must let go. Although it is very traumatic, I also believe that the owner should be there at the end; your cat needs you more than ever at that point. It is the owner's final act of selfless love for their cat who has given unconditional devotion to them throughout it's life. Vets and nurses are relative strangers to the cat - I always hold my cat and talk to them so that the experience is not a fearful one and the human they have trusted is with them at the end.

I did say previously that rarely do cats die in their sleep but I would like to tell the tale of Bob. Bob was a Usual Somali and when she was about thirteen years old, her owners decided they no longer wanted her. The Somali Welfare collected Bob and she was brought to the cattery to await re-homing. As luck would have it, an elderly gentleman who was well used to cats decided to offer her a home. All was fine for a few days but then Bob decided that this home was not for her and she attacked the poor man. She was returned to the cattery and we began to look for another home. This time, we found a couple who were used to feral cats; Bob lasted only two hours in the home before she sent both of them to Casualty! She was returned to the cattery once again but now we had a dilemma. We could not risk re-homing her a third time as she obviously had issues; uprooted from her original home, this was an elderly cat set in her ways.

Each day, I spent time with her in the pen and then she pushed her luck by deciding to give me a trip to Casualty. Fortunately for me, I was well padded and as she curled all four paws round my arm whilst at the same time trying to deploy her teeth, I unceremoniously flung her off. The look of disbelief on her face was evident and I told her in no uncertain terms that her behaviour was totally unacceptable. Somalis are bright little buttons and she knew she had met her match. Re-homing was out of the question and so she joined my little band of rescues on the farm. The other rescues were not impressed by the new addition to the ranks and Bob spent most of her time in the fields or with the chickens. Fizz, in particular, hated her with a passion. I tried to tell him that just as he had suffered in the past, so had the new addition, but he would have none of it. Over the months, they worked out a territory on the farm between themselves, but woe betide Bob if she ever crossed over the invisible line and entered Fizz's domain.

Matters were resolved in an unexpected way. Bob was now a typical Somali - very friendly and confident and she had begun to follow me around the farm (as long as Fizz was not in sight). I decided to clear the bottom of my fish pond; Fizz, as per usual, was in attendance in a supervisory capacity. Bob was curious as to what I was doing so came along to investigate; the next moment, the two of them were hurling themselves through the air with fur flying everywhere. I didn't think twice but threw the contents of my net over the pair of them! The fight stopped immediately; the two cats were covered in the disgusting sludge from the pond. They gave me the most withering look and then proceeded to clean each other, interspersed with steely glares in my direction. They united against the common enemy – me! From that point on, they lived in harmony.

Bob thrived on the farm; at last she had found the home that suited her. The bad behaviour was a thing of the past and for many years she lived happily.

As the years rolled by, she began to experience many conditions suffered by elderly cats but regular trips to the vet kept her bobbing along. One morning, when I went to feed the rescues, none appeared, which was most unusual. I went to their beds and found Fizz sitting vigil with Bob who had passed away in the night. As soon as I arrived, Fizz left her side and continued the business of his day. I buried Bob on the farm where she had spent her twilight years and had blossomed in to a true Somali.

Chapter 13. The Somali Cat Club

If you own a Somali then do join the Somali Cat Club. The Club was founded in 1981 and is the guardian of the breed; aims include safeguarding the well-being of Somali cats and promoting the purity of the breed. Throughout this book, I have taken great care not to mention any prefixes. Serious breeders purchase from the GCCF a prefix that is unique to them; all the cats they breed carry that prefix before their names. Once a prefix has been bought, no one else can use it and the breeder becomes identified with the prefix. All the cats in this book have been referred to by their pet names because I firmly believe that no prefix is more important than the breed or the Club. It is the role of the Club to encourage the improvement of type and colour and the Club sets the Standard of Points which cannot be altered without the agreement of the membership at an AGM. The Club has a committee which meets on a regular basis, made up of twelve elected committee members, each has a designated role. Apart from the officers of the Club, there is a welfare officer, someone responsible for advertising/sponsorship, membership and cup secretaries. All the committee members are volunteers and fit in the work they do for the Club around their busy lives.

The Somali Cat Club is always working to widen the appreciation of Somalis. At many shows throughout the year you will see the Somali stand where you can buy all manner of Club and cat related items. If you are very lucky, you may be able to purchase a chocolate cake, legendary in the Cat Fancy, made by our present welfare officer, Mrs Alison Lyall. The Somali Cat Club also puts Somalis on exhibition at shows; these cats are not in competition but there for the public to meet and handle, whilst at the same time learning a little about our breed. Over many years, the Club has supported exhibition pens at The Supreme Cat show, The National and in recent years, the London Pet Show. The production of this book has been a team effort with committee members helping in various ways. The Club provides information for members and has a website where all manner of information can be found at **www.somalicatclub.com**. On the site you will find information about the breed, pictures of numerous Somalis, how to locate a breeder and a list of kittens available for sale. The Club also produces a journal annually which is packed full of information about forthcoming events, past successes and tales of much loved Somalis written by their owners. I belong to a number of cat clubs but I can honestly say that the Somali Cat Club is one of the friendliest; experienced Somali breeders and owners are only too willing to give advice and help to members who may be having problems.

The Club holds a breed show annually. At this show, you will see more Somalis under one roof than at any other show. Once again, the committee work extremely hard to make the day a success. The show is always held on the third Saturday in March and over the years we have had some very eventful shows. The highlight of the day is when the Overall Best Exhibit is chosen. Any breeder will admit that to winning that accolade at the breed show is one of the best results they will ever get.

Each year the Club holds an AGM. This is not just a business meeting, but a social gathering as well. The committee provide the lunch and all members are welcome to attend. Once the business is over, trophies and awards are presented. Throughout the year, cats that have been shown gain points for their success, the show record forms are sent to the cup secretary and according to how well they have done, they are presented with the relevant trophy. There are two awards which are particularly prized. The first is the Muriel Harvey Award. Muriel was a breeder of Somalis, and even to this day, when I look at my kittens, I remember the look that Muriel's had; she bred cats to an incredible standard and her show presentation was second to none. She was not only a successful breeder but also for some time Chairman of the Club. Muriel gave a great deal to the breed and the Club and, in memory of her, it was decided to make an award annually to the person who has done most for the breed during the previous year. The award is not a trophy but a beautiful watercolour, by the well known feline artist, Kay Young, of a Usual Somali bred by Muriel. Members who receive this award consider it a great honour, with the additional bonus that it can adorn their home for a year! The second award is the Anne Rickson Trophy. Anne was a very senior judge of all breeds but she was always very interested and supportive of the work of the Somali Cat Club. This award is presented to the cat who has done the most for the breed. It is most unusual that this is awarded to a show cat; quite rightly, it tends to go to a cat who, by whatever means, has had an impact on the Club or the breed. One such recipient was a cat called Gypsy.

In 2008 Gypsy's owners no longer wanted her so they contacted the Somali Cat Club for help. Fortunately, we were able to find a home for her very promptly but, before she went to her new home, she was involved in a road traffic accident. Her fragile body was hit by a car and the prognosis was extremely poor as her tail had been broken very close to the base and she had also suffered damage to the bowel and bladder. The owners were unable to pay for veterinary treatment and nor were they prepared to nurse this very sick cat. The Club decided she should be brought to me and I would take care of her and at least give her a chance that her injuries might heal.

This was a long protracted case and the vet bills incurred were substantial; true to form, the Somali Cat Club went into action. At any show where we had a Club stall, we busied ourselves with raising funds to cover Gypsy's expenses. We sold badges with her picture and a logo stating 'We are supporting Gypsy'; for months, it was impossible go to a show without seeing people (who were not even involved in our breed) sporting the badges. Not only did Gypsy's plight unite all Somali owners but also the Cat Fancy in general. With careful nursing, finally the bowel and bladder recovered and the next stage was to amputate the tail which hung from her body like a broken twig. My vet did a wonderful job, managing to amputate it well away from the base so that the operation, although needing considerable skill, was not as complicated as we had first thought.

Gypsy thrived; she was a delightful cat and the welfare officer set about finding her a suitable home. Finally, as almost always seems to be the case, the right home came along where Gypsy could roam free but at the same time be safe from road traffic. Her new owners were delighted with her and she is still living life to the full. Because Gypsy had done so much to bring out the very best in the Cat Fancy, she was awarded the Anne Rickson trophy for that year.

One of the most important roles of the Club is in the work it does for the welfare of Somalis. It is a myth that because a cat is a pedigree, it will never end up being unwanted and unloved. There are a number of reasons why a Somali may need to be re-homed and the saddest cases are those where the owner has died or is too ill to continue to look after the cat. These situations are unavoidable and the Club actively seeks new homes for the cats that are deprived of the humans they have loved and have loved them. The Club tries wherever possible to re-home directly from present home to new home as this is less stressful for the cat, but emergency situations do arise. For many years, any Somali who needed immediate care and accommodation came to my cattery. Usually, I only have the difficult cases, generally those with medical problems or temperament issues. Some stay a few weeks, others for many months and some never leave me, but almost always, as soon as the Somali is rehabilitated we look for a new home.

Finding the right home is crucial; after so much upheaval in a cat's life, we owe it to them to get it right. One such case was Cookie, a dear Usual Tortie Somali who had suffered an injury to the roof of her mouth which had caused permanent damage to the hard palate. Ironically, this meant that when she was happy and purring she produced copious amounts of saliva which drenched everyone and everything in range. After extensive tests, it was decided that her problem was inoperable; Alison found a possible new home and the prospective owners came to visit her. I always leave possible new owners with the cat and observe from a distance their reaction and, more importantly, the reaction of the cat. Cookie made such a fuss of them and showered them with her saliva which did not go down well at all - they were still prepared to give her a home but I knew they weren't the right owners and would have soon tired of her. I politely told them that in the long term I did not think she was suitable for them and they went home cat-less! Many weeks later, Alison sent a young couple to meet Cookie. Once again she showered them in saliva but this time the reaction was totally different as the man unceremoniously wiped his saliva sodden hands on his jeans; Cookie had found her new family! The Club received regular updates about Cookie's antics and she was a much loved cat.

It had always been a worry that if a Somali needed help in the summer months when my cattery is full of boarders, there would be nowhere for them to go. This worry was removed by an unbelievable series of events. The two little imps who had caused such chaos at the hotel in Chester were the much loved pets of Colin and Jo Hubert. I spoke to them often on the phone and they would tell me about all the antics of their cats. Some years ago Jo died but Colin continued to look after the cats and at intervals rang for advice. In 2011 Colin passed away; before his death, Jo Jo had also died but Harley was still alive, although not a well cat. After speaking to Colin's relatives and on the advice of the vet, it was decided Harley should be put to sleep rather than return to live with me; the stress for such an elderly sick cat would be too much for him.

Months after Colin's death, I received a phone call from a solicitor informing me that the Club had been left some money in Colin's will. I was delighted to think that their Somalis had given them so much pleasure that they wanted to help less fortunate souls. It was in passing that I asked how much money had been left; I expected £50 or even £100 - when I was told £10,000 I shrieked down the phone 'How much?!' This wonderful gesture has secured the future for Somalis needing immediate help. Some of the money was spent in constructing a purpose built unit of two rescue pens

MAUND BRYAN HOUSE
In memory of
Colin and Jo Hubert
Whose kind donation made it possible

and we had a grand opening in May 2012. We named the unit Maund Bryan because this was the name of Colin and Jo's house where they spent many happy years. Their legacy has already enabled the Club achieve a huge amount for the welfare of Somalis in need and it will continue to do so for many years to come; it is only fitting that I have dedicated this book in part to the memory of Colin and Jo.

The Club will help any Somali in need, even if the owner or breeder is not a member of the Club. As I said earlier, sometimes the cats who come in for rescue never leave me; this is the tale of my Three MusKATeers. One spring, I received a call from Alison informing me that Cat Protection had been involved in a most distressing rescue of fourteen Somalis, three of which were entire males who were completely wild. Cat Protection had no facilities for them, nor could they handle them. As I have worked with feral cats before, I agreed they should come to the farm and I would see if they could be tamed.

They arrived a couple of days later after being neutered by CP. When CP collected them from their previous home, they had all been living together in one pen so I decided to start them off together in a boarding pen. The gentleman who delivered them was very frosty in his attitude towards me and I felt embarrassed that a Somali breeder had brought us into such disrepute. I tried to assure him that this was not the norm for Somali breeders and when we took the cats to their new pen, he did admit that they would think they had arrived at the Ritz in comparison with their previous living quarters.

We knew very little about them, their ages were suspect and they had no names. I emailed Alison and told her they had arrived safely and gave her my first impressions; I wrote – one terrified, one shell shocked and one with attitude. How right I was. It was not long before I gave them names to suit their personalities - you will have to forgive me if you take offence at the names I chose! 'Shell shocked' became Fella because he was a sweetie, 'terrified' became Boris, after Boris Johnson, because you never knew quite how he was going to react and 'one with attitude' became Blair, after Tony Blair, because he couldn't to be trusted not to attack!

When they arrived they were under weight and generally in poor condition. I went out and bought a bag of the cheapest cat biscuits (which normally I would never use) because to give them top grade feed would have caused severe stomach upsets. For the first two weeks they had cheap, cheerful and plentiful food and gradually they were introduced to top quality feed, with no side effects. They had not been used to litter trays and initially they soiled anywhere and everywhere, but they soon got the hang of a dirt box.

Each day I would sit on the pen floor, chatting to them and trying to gain their trust, but they huddled up in the corner, terrified of human contact. Fella was the first to let me touch him, followed a few days later by Boris. Blair was having none of it and he was now becoming a problem; his refusal to be touched was unnerving Fella and Boris, so with great difficulty I moved them into an adjoining pen, leaving Blair on his own. By now they had been with me for nearly six weeks and they needed to be vaccinated. There wasn't a hope in hell that I could take them to my vet, so it was agreed that when Steph (one of the vets at my practice) came to board her own cat, she would vaccinate them. The day came: Steph arrived, armed with a crush cage and vaccine. I cannot begin to describe what a horrific time that was. We managed to do Fella and Boris but they were so upset by the procedure that I felt the little trust they had built up was destroyed, and as for Blair, he was manic. We did manage to get him in the crush cage but blood splattered everywhere as he frantically tried to escape, damaging his face in the process. Had the breeder who had done this to these cats turned up then, I think I would be in Holloway now, doing time! By the time we had finished, both Steph and I were visibly upset and I had three traumatised cats.

As far as I was concerned, worse was to come; they needed the second part of their vaccinations in three weeks time and I dreaded the thought.

However, over the succeeding weeks I gained the trust of Fella and Boris to such an extent that when Chris came out to do the second vaccination, I could hold them in my arms and they didn't feel a thing. Blair was another matter altogether; once again the crush cage was employed and I then made the decision that Blair could never be re-homed; he was too wild, so whilst he was in the crush cage, I moved him into a temporary pen in the barn. The idea was that, after a couple of weeks, he would be set free on the farm and the rest was up to him. I have had numerous feral cats on the farm from rescue organisations and surprisingly, none have ever left me once set free. I felt that Blair could be the exception. By now, Fella was virtually a normal Somali and although Boris was still tentative, he took his lead from Fella. I was confident that in time they could be re-homed together, but Boris wasn't quite ready. I spoke to Alison and told her of my fears that Blair, once freed, would be gone, so it was decided to encourage him to stay; Fella and Boris would be given the freedom of the farm during the day time and penned at night.

The boys loved their urban jungle, hunting, playing and meeting the customers. The day came for me to open Blair's pen and give him his freedom. He did what I had hoped and clambered into the roof rafters of the barn and then for some weeks he led a shadowy existence, although from afar I saw him scuttle into his feeding station for his meals. Slowly at feed times I got closer and closer until at last he allowed me to stroke his head.

September came and so did the committee meeting. The future of Boris and Fella had to be decided. I have looked after a number of waifs for the Somali Cat Club and fallen for quite a few of them but they always go to new homes if at all possible. My head said that Fella and Boris should go, as we never know when a Somali will arrive who, like Blair, will never tolerate a normal home environment, and I have only so much space for those unfortunate souls. But my heart said they should stay; Fella would fit in anywhere but Boris has a different temperament and I feared that he might revert back to wild and then, if he was returned, he would never truly trust me again. To my great relief, Alison decided they were happy here

The Somali Cat

and so they could stay. When I put them away that night, I told them I was no longer auntie but now I was their new mum and they were here to stay; not that they understood any of that, they just tucked into their tea!

What of Blair? We had further mountains to climb together. Hurdles came along and we just about scrambled over them. As the months passed, I was able to pick him up and he talked to me and ran to greet me in the morning and at night. Blair was becoming daily more confident but after he had been with me for just over a year, he suffered a thrombosis and had to be put to sleep. It is documented that cats have a memory of three years; I was devastated that Blair would not have had the time to forget his previous miserable existence; I felt that both he and I had been robbed.

Make no mistake, these three boys were both physically and mentally damaged by their upbringing. Please, if you breed Somalis, be very careful to whom you sell them. The breeder of these cats is known to the Club but not a member and this is not the first time she has caused anguish to cats and depleted the rescue funds of the Club. I hope that this is the last we shall ever hear of her but I have my doubts. Fella, Boris and I made an appearance at a show with the Somali Cat Club table to illustrate the work the Club does for those Somalis who are unfortunate enough to fall on hard times. They continue to live happily on the farm, greeting the customers and ruling their kingdom with velvet paws.

If you feel at any time you could offer a rescue Somali a loving, understanding, permanent home then please contact the Somali Cat Club. The Somali Cat Club is the only Club in Britain which caters solely for the Somali breed.

Chapter 14. New Horizons

The Somali Cat Club is a progressive Club and as has been illustrated in a previous chapter, it has embraced DNA testing. The health of the Somali is paramount in any breeding programme and to maintain the health and improve the vigour of the breed, the Club has always supported ways to widen the gene pool. With this in mind, the Club has worked hard to further the progression of Shorthaired Somalis.

There is nothing new about the Shorthaired Somali as they date back to the very beginning of the breed. The Somali originated from Abyssinian cats because some of them carried the longhair gene. No one knows for sure when this gene was introduced in to the Abyssinian breed, but possibly it came from out-crossing to domestic shorthairs, as this gene is present in the general population of non - pedigree cats and can be carried by shorthair cats. Until recently, Shorthair Somalis were referred to as Somali Variants. Variants have been used in Somali breeding programmes from the beginning; they are very useful because they enable the gene pool to be widened whilst not compromising on type or colour. The coat of the Shorthair should be of a medium length that is smooth, fine and dense but close lying. The coat should be of fairly uniform length with no ruff, toe

tufts, breeches or brush. A coat which is coarse or overly resilient is a serious fault as it is one of the significant differences between the desired coat quality of the Abyssinian and the shorthaired Somali. To maintain the correct coat quality, Shorthair Somalis must be mated to semi longhaired Somalis.

Preliminary recognition for the shorthair was granted in February 2012. Until then, the shorthairs could be bred from but not shown. The shorthair made its show debut at the Somali Cat Club Show in March 2012 where 4 shorthairs were shown who all gained their merits. At least 10 cats must gain 4 merits each from different judges to enable the breed to progress to Championship status. As I write, I am pleased to say that we have 9 cats who have fulfilled the criteria and we need one more. It is my fervent hope that we will achieve Championship status during 2014.

The shorthair has a great deal to offer the breed, but they are slightly different in temperament from the Longhaired Somalis. They are into everything at break neck speed; they are as quick as greased lightning through doors and are extremely agile. They lack the wisdom of the longhair and will rush in where angels fear to tread, but they are equally as loving with a huge sense of humour; rather like cream cakes, they are naughty but nice! For some people, the major advantage they have over the longhair is that their coat is extremely easy to care for. Somali lovers fazed by the longer coat can now have a cat with all the Somali attributes in a short coat. Short haired Somalis will eventually be available in all of the 28 colours; by using short haired Somalis in out-crossing programmes, breeders are able to maintain a healthy gene pool whilst protecting the priorities of the breed.

I hope this book has given you some insight into this wonderful breed. It is very difficult to put into words the incredible character of the Somali. For me, the cover cat, Cherub, epitomises the Somali breed. She is a stunning Usual with appealing and expressive eyes which have the ability to look deep into your soul. Her face is framed by a magnificent ruff and gives the impression of a miniature lion; I would advise anyone to 'let a little lion into your life' – you will never regret it! To end this book, I wondered how I could sum up adequately what it is like to live with a Somali but the solution came in an email from a besotted owner; it says it all!

From: Mary xxxxxx
Sent: 02 December 2013 19:34
To: xxxxxxxxxxxxxxx
Subject: Boogie Woogie

Dear Di

I thought you would like to know that Boogie Woogie (who is now called Beau, amongst other things – Buster, Oi You, etc.) is doing splendidly and has landed firmly on all four paws in Addlestone.

He attracts universal admiration – the vet asks if she may cuddle him first, my next door neighbours on both sides admire him open-mouthed, and as for the grandchildren and great-nieces and nephews – well! He sticks to my youngest grandson (now 16 months old) like glue. Finn (grandson) rushes into the house calling 'Beau, Beau'. They investigate the toy box together. Finn throws Beau's toys for him and he fetches them for Finn to throw again, he lets Finn cuddle him and stroke his tail – in short, they have a relationship which beggars belief. Everyone who sees them together says they have never seen a cat behave so amiably and companionably with a small child before.

We all adore him. He has the best tail I have ever clapped eyes on and my daughter would sneak him away with her to live with them if she thought she had the slightest chance of getting away with it.

Polly, my other cat who is a white and black moggie (stunning also, of course) and he get on really well. They rough and tumble and chase around sometimes, but the fur never flies and there is never any growling or spitting.

Beau is interested in everything which can be a pain – as soon as you start to do anything, he is there poking his nose in, which of course should be really annoying but we all think its charming. You have to be very careful because he shoots into cupboards and drawers etc. like greased lightning. My husband, who is very restrained in all his relationships, is completely besotted with Beau and tolerates a degree of interference in the workshop which I would not have believed possible.

Beau is now all vaccinated, chipped and neutered and growing into the most beautiful cat. I am confident he would sweep the board if I showed him, but I am not going to. I would never have believed that a breed of cat could trump my affection for Burmese and Siamese, but I have to say Beau has done that.

In short, we adore him and once I have worked out how to get the photos from my phone onto the computer, I will send you some pictures. You may yet get to see him again however, as at some point if I am stuck for boarding him and Polly if we ever go away again, I may well be asking you to have him.

Thank you very much indeed, Di.
With very kind regards
Mary

On Dec 2, 2013 8:35 PM, "Dianne Taylor" wrote:
Hi I am so pleased that all are enchanted by him but I must take little credit as he is typical of the breed. I look forward to some photos and it would be great to see him one day in the flesh again. Thank you for giving him the type of home a Somali thrives in. Best of luck when you put up the Xmas tree!!! Di

Appendix 1. The GCCF Standard of Points

SOMALI – 63L & 63S

General Type Standard

The Somali should be a beautifully balanced cat of medium build and foreign type; the head to be broad and curving to a firm wedge set on an elegant neck; the body to be firm, lithe and muscular of medium length, tail fairly long and gently tapering. The head, body, legs, feet and tail should be in proportion, giving a well-balanced appearance with no exaggerated features. The expression should be alert and smiling. The cat should be in excellent physical condition with good weight for its size.

Head - A moderate wedge with brow, cheek and profile lines showing gently rounded contours. There should be a slight rise from the bridge of the nose to the forehead which should be high with good width between the ears. From the front, a shallow indentation should form the muzzle. In profile, a slight nose break is essential, a firm chin and an elegant neck.

Ears - Set wide apart but not low, broad at the base, proportionately large, pricked well-cupped and tufted. Inner edges well furnished with long hair.

Eyes - Large, almond-shaped, set obliquely and well apart, expressive and bright. Accentuated by a dark surround encircled by lighter coloured "spectacles". Short dark "pencil" lines at either edge of the eye, the inner one vertical, the outer one pointing towards the ear. Colour: amber, hazel or green: the richer and deeper the better.

Body - Firm, lithe and muscular of medium size, foreign type with a level back.

Legs and Feet - Long legs. Feet oval with tufts between the toes <u>on the 63L</u>.

Tail –
63L Long, well furnished, broad at the base and tapering slightly with a full brush. Length to balance with the body.
63S Long, thick at the base and tapering slightly to a rounded tip. Length to balance with the body.

Coat –

63L Soft and fine, dense but lying flat along the spine. Semi- long, except over the shoulders where a shorter length is permitted. All other points being equal, preference should be given to the cat with a ruff and full breeches. Ruff and breeches may not be apparent in kittens.

63S A coat of medium length that is smooth, fine and dense but close lying. The coat will be of fairly uniform length with no ruff, toe tufts, breeches or brush.

A coarse or overly resilient coat in the shorthaired Somali is to be considered a serious fault.

Colour and Pattern - Ticking is the essence of the Somali coat. On the 63L there should be at least three bands on every hair, i.e. six contrasting colour sections from base hair to tip. On the 63S there should be at least two bands on every hair i.e. four contrasting colour sections from base hair to tip. On both coat lengths the roots should be the colour of the base hair and the final band must be the ticking colour.

Ticking is slow to develop but should be apparent at least on the shoulders of all kittens.

Ear tips and tufts, facial markings, top and tip of tail, toe tufts and heels are the same colour as the ticking. Darker shading along the spine and top of tail is desirable.

Chest, belly, under tail, inside of legs and breeches are the colour of the unmarked base hair.

Depth of colour in sex-linked colours may not be achieved in kittens or young cats as this develops with maturity.

Withhold all Awards for:
1. White locket or white patches anywhere except around the chin, lips and nostrils.
2. Absence of ticking in adults.
3. Unbroken necklace.

Withhold Certificates or First Prizes in Kitten Open Classes for:
1. Cobby or oriental type.
2. Pinched or fine muzzle.
3. Straight profile or stop.
4. Absence of facial markings
5. Incorrectly coloured heels. (Heel colour in silvers may not extend to the hock).

6. Severe barring on legs, body or tail.
7. A coarse or overly resilient coat in shorthaired Somalis.
8. Any defects as listed in the Preface to the SOP booklet.

SCALE OF POINTS – 63L

Head...	15
Ears...	10
Eyes...	10
Body...	10
Legs and Feet...	5
Tail...	5
Coat - Colour...	15
- Ticking...	15
- Texture...	5
- Length	10
	Total 100

SCALE OF POINTS – 63S

Head...	15
Ears...	10
Eyes...	10
Body...	10
Legs and Feet...	5
Tail...	5
Coat - Colour...	15
- Ticking...	15
- Texture...	10
- Length...	5
	Total 100

USUAL (63L; 63S)

Overall impression: a rich golden brown made up of an apricot base coat ticked with black.

Ticking, ear tips and tufts, facial markings, top and tip of tail, toe tufts and heels: Black

Chest, belly, under tail, inside of legs and breeches: Rich apricot - colour should be as rich as possible.

Nose leather: Tile red.

Paw pads: Black or brown.

Withhold Certificates or First Prizes in Kitten Open Classes for (additional to General Type Standard):
1. Cold, pale tone to the coat
2. Grey roots extending over a large area of the body. (Seasonal darkening at the roots during change of coat should not be penalised) *(this amendment Council October 2009)*
3. All other withholding faults as in the Somali General Type Standard.

SORREL (63La; 63Sa)

Overall impression: a rich copper colour made up of an apricot base coat ticked with cinnamon.

Ticking, **ear tips and tufts, facial markings, top and tip of tail, toe tufts and heels:** Cinnamon.

Chest, belly, under tail, inside of legs and breeches: Rich apricot.

Nose leather and paw pads: Pink.

Withhold Certificates or First Prizes in Kitten Open Classes for (additional to General Type Standard):
1. Absence of contrast between the undercoat and ticking.
2. All other withholding faults as in the Somali General Type Standard.

CHOCOLATE (63Lb; 63Sb)

Overall impression: a rich, warm chestnut brown made up of an apricot base coat ticked with dark chocolate.

Ticking, ear tips and tufts, facial markings, top and tip of tail, toe tufts and heels: Dark chocolate.

Chest, belly, under tail, inside of legs and breeches: Rich apricot.

Nose leather: Pinkish chocolate

Paw pads: Chocolate or rosy, pinkish chocolate

Withhold Certificates or First Prizes in Kitten Open Classes for (additional to General Type Standard):
1. Absence of contrast sufficient to obscure ticking.
2. All other withholding faults as in the Somali General Type Standard.

BLUE (63Lc; 63Sc)
Overall impression: a soft blue consisting of a warm oatmeal or mushroom base coat ticked with any shade of blue.
Ticking, ear tips and tufts, facial markings, top and tip of tail, toe tufts and heels: Blue.
Chest, belly, under tail, inside of legs and breeches: Warm mushroom.
Nose leather and paw pads: Mauvish blue.

Withhold Certificates or First Prizes in Kitten Open Classes for (additional to General Type Standard):
1. White undercoat anywhere on the body: this is particularly obvious on the back.
2. All other withholding faults as in the Somali General Type Standard.

LILAC (63Ld; 63Sd)
Overall impression: a warm dove grey made up of an oatmeal or mushroom undercoat ticked with lilac.
Ticking, ear tips and tufts, facial markings, top and tip of tail, toe tufts and heels: Lilac.
Chest, belly, under tail, inside of legs and breeches: Mushroom.
Nose leather and paw pads: Mauvish pink.

Withhold Certificates or First Prizes in Kitten Open Classes for (additional to General Type Standard):
1. Absence of contrast sufficient to obscure ticking.
2. All other withholding faults as in the Somali General Type Standard.

FAWN (63Le; 63Se)
Overall impression: a warm powdery fawn made up of a pale oatmeal or mushroom undercoat ticked with fawn.
Ticking, ear tips and tufts, facial markings, top and tip of tail, toe tufts and heels: Fawn.
Chest, belly, under tail, inside of legs and breeches: Pale mushroom.
Nose leather: Pink
Paw pads: Mauvish pink.

Withhold Certificates or First Prizes in Kitten Open Classes for (additional to General Type Standard):
1. Absence of contrast sufficient to obscure ticking.
2. All other withholding faults as in the Somali General Type Standard.

RED (63Lf; 63Sf)

Overall impression: A warm, glowing red made up of pale red clearly ticked with a deeper tone of red.

Ticking, ear tips and tufts, facial markings, top and tip of tail, toe tufts and heels: Bright red.

Chest, belly, under tail, inside of legs and breeches: A paler shade of red.

Nose leather and paw pads: Bright pink.

Note: Freckles may occur on nose, lips, eyelids, ears and paw pads. Slight freckling should not be penalised.

Withhold Certificates or First Prizes in Kitten Open Classes for (additional to General Type Standard):
1. Absence of contrast sufficient to obscure ticking.
2. All other withholding faults as in the Somali General Type Standard.

CREAM (63Lg; 63Sg)

Overall impression: A soft, warm, powdery effect made up of a pale cream clearly ticked with a rich cream.

Ticking, ear tips and tufts, facial markings, top and tip of tail, toe tufts and heels: Rich cream.

Chest, belly, under tail, inside of legs and breeches: A paler shade of cream.

Nose leather: Creamy pink

Paw pads: Flesh pink.

Note: Freckles may occur on nose, lips, eyelids, ears and paw pads. Slight freckling should not be penalised.

Withhold Certificates or First Prizes in Kitten Open Classes for (additional to General Type Standard):
1. Absence of contrast sufficient to obscure ticking.
2. All other withholding faults as in the Somali General Type Standard.

TORTIE SOMALI

Colour distribution is random and immaterial though a solid foot is not permissible. Ticking, ear tips and tufts, facial markings, top and tip of tail, toe tufts and heels to be a mingling of the standard ticking colour and that determined by the sex-linked gene. Chest, belly, under tail, inside of legs and breeches to be a mingling of the standard base coat colour and that determined by the sex-linked gene. Presence or absence of a blaze is immaterial.

Withhold Certificates or First Prizes in Kitten Open Classes for (additional to General Type Standard):
1. Solid foot
2. Absence of contrast sufficient to obscure ticking.

USUAL TORTIE (63Lt; 63St)
Overall impression: A mixture of rich, golden brown ticked with black and reddish apricot ticked with red.
Ticking, ear tips and tufts, facial markings, top and tip of tail, toe tufts and heels: A mingling of black and bright red.
Chest, belly, under tail, inside of legs and breeches: A mingling of apricot and red.
Nose leather: Red and/or pink
Paw pads: Black and/or pink.

Withhold Certificates or First Prizes in Kitten Open Classes for (additional to General Type Standard):
1. Grey roots extending over a large area of the body. (Seasonal darkening at the roots during change of coat should not be penalised).

SORREL TORTIE (63Lat; 63Sat)
Overall impression: A mixture of lustrous copper ticked with cinnamon and reddish apricot ticked with red.
Ticking, ear tips and tufts, facial markings, top and tip of tail, toe tufts and heels: A mingling of cinnamon and bright red.
Chest, belly, under tail, inside of legs and breeches: A mingling of apricot and red.
Nose leather and paw pads: Pink and/or red

CHOCOLATE TORTIE (63Lbt; 63Sbt)
Overall impression: A mixture of rich, warm chestnut brown ticked with dark chocolate and reddish apricot ticked with red.
Ticking, ear tips and tufts, facial markings, top and tip of tail, toe tufts and heels: A mingling of dark chocolate and bright red.
Chest, belly, under tail, inside of legs and breeches: A mingling of apricot and red.
Nose leather and paw pads: Chocolate and/or red or rosy, pinkish chocolate and/or red.

BLUE TORTIE (63Lct; 63Sct)
Overall impression: A mixture of soft, warm blue ticked with a deeper blue-grey and pale cream ticked with a rich cream.
Ticking, ear tips and tufts, facial markings, top and tip of tail, toe tufts and heels: A mingling of blue and rich cream.
Chest, belly, under tail, inside of legs and breeches: A mingling of warm mushroom and pale cream.
Nose leather and paw pads: Mauvish blue and/or pink

LILAC TORTIE (63Ldt; 63Sdt)
Overall impression: A mixture of warm, dove grey ticked with a deeper dove grey and pale cream ticked with a rich cream.
Ticking, ear tips and tufts, facial markings, top and tip of tail, toe tufts and heels: A mingling of lilac and rich cream.
Chest, belly, under tail, inside of legs and breeches: A mingling of mushroom and pale cream.
Nose leather and paw pads: Mauvish pink and/or pink

FAWN TORTIE (63Let; 63Set)
Overall impression: A mixture of warm, powdery fawn ticked with a deeper fawn and pale cream ticked with a rich cream.
Ticking, ear tips and tufts, facial markings, top and tip of tail, toe tufts and heels: A mingling of warm fawn and rich cream.
Chest, belly, under tail, inside of legs and breeches: A mingling of pale mushroom and pale cream.
Nose leather and paw pads: Mauvish pink and/or pink

SILVER SOMALI

The base hair of all this group should be silvery white giving an overall lustrous, silvery sheen. Ticking, ear tips and tufts, facial markings, top and tip of tail, toe tufts and heels to be the same colour as in the appropriate non-silver variety. Chest, belly, under tail, inside of legs and breeches to be silvery white.

Withhold Certificates or First Prizes in Kitten Open Classes for (additional to General Type Standard):
1. Tarnishing over a substantial portion of the designated silver areas. (Minor patches of tarnishing are not to be considered a fault if the overall impression is of silver.)

USUAL SILVER (63Ls; 63Ss)
Overall impression: A clear silver ticked with black
Ticking, ear tips and tufts, facial markings, top and tip of tail, toe tufts and heels: Black
Chest, belly, under tail, inside of legs and breeches: Silvery white
Nose leather: Brick red
Paw pads: Black or brown.

SORREL SILVER (63Las; 63Sas)
Overall impression: A soft, silvery peach ticked with cinnamon.
Ticking, ear tips and tufts, facial markings, top and tip of tail, toe tufts and heels: Cinnamon.
Chest, belly, under tail, inside of legs and breeches: Silvery white
Nose leather and paw pads: Pink

CHOCOLATE SILVER (63Lbs; 63Sbs)
Overall impression: A cool, silvery brown ticked with dark chocolate.
Ticking, ear tips and tufts, facial markings, top and tip of tail, toe tufts and heels: Dark chocolate
Chest, belly, under tail, inside of legs and breeches: Silvery white
Nose leather and paw pads: Chocolate or rosy, pinkish chocolate

BLUE SILVER (63Lcs; 63Scs)
Overall impression: A glacial, silvery blue ticked with darker blue.
Ticking, ear tips and tufts, facial markings, top and tip of tail, toe tufts and heels: Blue.

Chest, belly, under tail, inside of legs and breeches: Silvery white
Note: The base coat MUST be silvery white
Nose leather and paw pads: Mauvish blue.

LILAC SILVER (63Lds; 63Sds)

Overall impression: A frosty, silvery dove grey ticked with lilac.
Ticking, ear tips and tufts, facial markings, top and tip of tail, toe tufts and heels: Lilac
Chest, belly, under tail, inside of legs and breeches: Silvery white
Nose leather and paw pads: Mauvish pink.

FAWN SILVER (63Les; 63Ses)

Overall impression: A cool, silvery fawn ticked with a darker fawn.
Ticking, ear tips and tufts, facial markings, top and tip of tail, toe tufts and heels: Fawn
Chest, belly, under tail, inside of legs and breeches: Silvery white
Nose leather: Pink
Paw pads: Mauvish pink

RED SILVER (63Lfs; 63Sfs)

Overall impression: A clear, silvery red ticked with red.
Ticking, ear tips and tufts, facial markings, top and tip of tail, toe tufts and heels: Red
Chest, belly, under tail, inside of legs and breeches: Silvery white
Nose leather and paw pads: Bright pink
Note: Freckles may occur on nose, lips, eyelids, ears and paw pads. Slight freckling should not be penalised.

CREAM SILVER (63Lgs; 63Sgs)

Overall impression: A powdery, silvery cream ticked with rich cream.
Ticking, ear tips and tufts, facial markings, top and tip of tail, toe tufts and heels: Rich cream
Chest, belly, under tail, inside of legs and breeches: Silvery white
Nose leather: Creamy pink
Paw pads: Flesh pink
Note: Freckles may occur on nose, lips, eyelids, ears and paw pads. Slight freckling should not be penalised.

TORTIE SILVER SOMALIS

As for the Silver Somalis except that the silvery white base hair should have two colours of ticking: the standard colour and that expressing the sex-linked gene. The distribution of these two colours is immaterial but a solid foot is not permissible.

Withhold Certificates or First Prizes in Kitten Open Classes for (additional to General Type Standard): as for Silver Somalis above.

USUAL TORTIE SILVER (63Lts; 63Sts)
Overall impression: A mixture of clear silver ticked with black and silvery red ticked with red.
Ticking, ear tips and tufts, facial markings, top and tip of tail, toe tufts and heels: A mingling of black and red.
Chest, belly, under tail, inside of legs and breeches: Silvery white
Nose leather: Red and/or pink.
Paw pads: Black and/or pink.

SORREL TORTIE SILVER (63Lats; 63Sats)
Overall impression: A mixture of cool, silvery peach ticked with cinnamon and silvery red ticked with red.
Ticking, ear tips and tufts, facial markings, top and tip of tail, toe tufts and heels: A mingling of cinnamon and red.
Chest, belly, under tail, inside of legs and breeches: Silvery white
Nose leather and paw pads: Red and/or pink.

CHOCOLATE TORTIE SILVER (63Lbts; 63Sbts)
Overall impression: A mixture of cool, silvery brown ticked with dark chocolate and silvery red ticked with red.
Ticking, ear tips and tufts, facial markings, top and tip of tail, toe tufts and heels: A mingling of dark chocolate and red.
Chest, belly, under tail, inside of legs and breeches: Silvery white
Nose leather and paw pads: Pinkish chocolate and/or pink.

BLUE TORTIE SILVER (63Lcts; 63Scts)
Overall impression: A mixture of glacial, silvery blue ticked with blue and powdery, silvery cream ticked with rich cream.

Ticking, ear tips and tufts, facial markings, top and tip of tail, toe tufts and heels: A mingling of blue and rich cream.

Chest, belly, under tail, inside of legs and breeches: Silvery white

Nose leather and paw pads: Mauvish blue and/or pink.

LILAC TORTIE SILVER (63Ldts; 63Sdts)

Overall impression: A mixture of frosty, silvery dove grey ticked with lilac and powdery, silvery cream ticked with rich cream.

Ticking, ear tips and tufts, facial markings, top and tip of tail, toe tufts and heels: a mingling of lilac and rich cream.

Chest, belly, under tail, inside of legs and breeches: silvery white

Nose leather and paw pads: Mauvish pink and/or pink.

FAWN TORTIE SILVER (63Lets; 63Sets)

Overall impression: A mixture of cool, silvery fawn ticked with a darker fawn and powdery, silvery cream ticked with rich cream.

Ticking, ear tips and tufts, facial markings, top and tip of tail, toe tufts and heels: a mingling of warm fawn and rich cream.

Chest, belly, under tail, inside of legs and breeches: silvery white

Nose leather and paw pads: Mauvish pink and/or pink.

Please Note

Sometime during 2014 the Governing Council of the Cat Fancy (GCCF) will be changing all breed numbers over to the Easy Mind System (EMS codes).

The Somali Cat Club website will have a compete list of new EMS codes to use.

The GCCF website will also have a converter where you can insert your old breed number and it will generate the EMS code for you.

Appendix 2. Colour Mating Chart

The table on page 121 is a colour mating chart for Usual, Sorrel, Blue & Fawn Somalis, showing proportions of colours to be expected over a large number of repeat matings.

Key to colours:-U = Usual
                    B = Blue (Blue is dilute Usual)
                    S = Sorrel
                    F = Fawn (Fawn is dilute Sorrel)
                    d = dilute

Colours carried are shown in brackets, e.g:-
                    Usual carrying Sorrel = U(S)
                    Sorrel carrying dilute = S(d)

If Chocolate is introduced, similar results may be expected as for Sorrel, but it should be noted that Chocolate is dominant to Sorrel, and that Lilac (dilute Chocolate) is dominant to Fawn (dilute Sorrel). However, as both Sorrel and Chocolate can be carried as recessive factors, particular care should be taken when determining the correct colour of kittens.

If Silver is introduced (the Inhibitor gene being responsible for inhibiting the development of the undercoat) it should be remembered that the gene is dominant to "Non-Silver" (or Non-Inhibitor).

A Silver cat can be **homozygous** Silver (both sides of its genetic material being Silver) or **heterozygous** Silver (one Silver gene and one Non-Silver gene).
A Non-Silver cat therefore cannot carry Silver and will only produce Silver kittens when mated to a Silver.

A homozygous Silver cat can only ever produce the Silver genes and all its offspring will be Silver.

Here is a list to help:-

Non-Silver to Non-Silver	no Silver kittens
Heterozygous Silver to Non-Silver	½ Heterozygous Silver ½ Non-Silver
Heterozygous Silver to Heterozygous Silver	¼ Homozygous Silver ½ Heterozygous Silver ¼ Non-Silver
Homozygous Silver to Non-Silver	all Heterozygous Silver
Homozygous Silver to Heterozygous Silver	½ Heterozygous Silver ½ Homozygous Silver
Homozygous Silver to Homozygous Silver	all Homozygous Silver

	U	U(d)	U(S)	U(Sd)	B	B(S)	S	S(d)	F
U x U	All								
U x U(d)	1/2	1/2							
U x U(S)	1/2		1/2						
U x U(Sd)	1/4	1/4	1/4	1/4					
U x B		All							
U x B(S)		1/2		1/2					
U x S			All						
U x S(d)			1/2	1/2					
U x F				All					
U(S) x U(d)	1/4	1/4	1/4	1/4					
U(S) x U(S)	1/4		1/2				1/4		
U(S) x U(Sd)	1/8	1/8	1/4	1/4			1/8	1/8	
U(S) x B		1/2		1/2					
U(S) x B(S)		1/4		1/2				1/4	
U(S) x S			1/2				1/2		
U(S) x S(d)			1/4	1/4			1/4	1/4	
U(S) x F				1/2				1/2	
U(Sd) x U(d)	1/8	1/4	1/8	1/4	1/8	1/8			
U(Sd) x U(Sd)	1/16	1/8	1/8	1/4	1/16	1/8	1/16	1/8	1/16
U(Sd) x B		1/4		1/4	1/4	1/4			
U(Sd) x B(S)		1/8		1/4	1/8	1/4		1/8	1/8
U(Sd) x S			1/4	1/4			1/4	1/4	
U(Sd) x S(d)			1/8	1/4		1/8	1/8	1/4	1/8
U(Sd) x F				1/4		1/4		1/4	1/4
U(d) x U(d)	1/4	1/2			1/4				
U(d) x B		1/2			1/2				
U(d) x B(S)		1/4		1/4	1/4	1/4			
U(d) x S			1/2	1/2					
U(d)x S(d)			1/4	1/2		1/4			
U(d) x F				1/2		1/2			
B x B					All				
B x B(S)					1/2	1/2			
B x S			All						
B x S(d)				1/2		1/2			
B x F						All			
B(S) x B(S)					1/4	1/2			1/4
B(S) x S			1/2					1/2	
B(S) x S(d)				1/4		1/4		1/4	1/4
B(S) x F						1/2			1/2
S x S							All		
S x S(d)							1/2	1/2	
S x F								All	
S(d) x S(d)							1/4	1/2	1/4
Sd x F								1/2	1/2
F x F									All
	U	U(d)	U(S)	U(Sd)	B	B(S)	S	S(d)	F

Appendix 3. Gestation Table

This Table is based on a 365 day year and a 65 day gestation period

Mated	Pink up	Kittens due	9 weeks	12 weeks
1st January	22nd January	7th March	9th May	30th May
5th "	26th "	11th "	13th "	3rd June
9th "	30th "	15th "	17th "	7th "
13th "	3rd February	19th "	21st "	11th "
17th "	7th "	23rd "	25th "	15th "
21st "	11th "	27th "	29th "	19th "
25th "	15th "	31st "	2nd June	23rd "
29th "	19th "	4th April	6th "	27th "
2nd February	23rd "	8th "	10th "	1st July
6th "	27th "	12th "	14th "	5th "
10th "	3rd March	16th "	18th "	9th "
14th "	7th "	20th "	22nd "	13th "
18th "	11th "	24th "	26th "	17th "
22nd "	15th "	28th "	30th "	21st "
26th "	19th "	2nd May	4th July	25th "
2nd March	23rd "	6th "	8th "	29th "
6th "	27th "	10th "	12th "	2nd August
10th "	31st "	14th "	16th "	6th "
14th "	4th April	18th "	20th "	10th "
18th "	8th "	22nd "	24th "	14th "
22nd "	12th "	26th "	28th "	18th "
26th "	16th "	30th "	1st August	22nd "
30th "	20th "	3rd June	5th "	26th "
3rd April	24th "	7th "	9th "	30th "
7th "	28th "	11th "	13th "	3rd September
11th "	2nd May	15th "	17th "	7th "
15th "	6th "	19th "	21st "	11th "
19th "	10th "	23rd "	25th "	15th "
23rd "	14th "	27th "	29th "	19th "

Mated	Pink up	Kittens due	9 weeks	12 weeks
27th April	18th May	1st July	2nd September	23rd September
1st May	22nd "	5th "	6th "	27th "
5th "	26th "	9th "	10th "	1st October
9th "	30th "	13th "	14th "	5th "
13th "	3rd June	17th "	18th "	9th "
17th "	7th "	21st "	22nd "	13th "
21st "	11th "	25th "	26th "	17th "
25th "	15th "	29th "	30th "	21st "
29th "	19th "	2nd August	4th October	25th "
2nd June	23rd "	6th "	8th "	29th "
6th "	27th "	10th "	12th "	2nd November
10th "	1st July	14th "	16th "	6th "
14th "	5th "	18th "	20th "	10th "
18th "	9th "	22nd "	24th "	14th "
22nd "	13th "	26th "	28th "	18th "
26th "	17th "	30th "	1st November	22nd "
30th "	21st "	3rd September	5th "	26th "
4th July	25th "	7th "	9th "	30th "
8th "	29th "	11th "	13th "	4th December
12th "	2nd August	15th "	17th "	8th "
16th "	6th "	19th "	21st "	12th "
20th "	10th "	23rd "	25th "	16th "
24th "	14th "	27th "	29th "	20th "
28th "	18th "	1st October	3rd December	24th "
1st August	22nd "	5th "	7th "	28th "
5th "	26th "	9th "	11th "	1st January
9th "	30th "	13th "	15th "	5th "
13th "	3rd September	17th "	19th "	9th "
17th "	7th "	21st "	23rd "	13th "
21st "	11th "	25th "	27th "	17th "
25th "	15th "	29th "	31st "	21st "
29th "	19th "	2nd "	4th "	25th "

Mated	Pink up	Kittens due	9 weeks	12 weeks
2nd September	23rd September	6th November	8th January	29th January
6th "	27th "	10th "	12th "	2nd February
10th "	1st October	14th "	16th "	6th "
14th "	5th "	18th "	20th "	10th "
18th "	9th "	22nd "	24th "	14th "
22nd "	13th "	26th "	28th "	18th "
26th "	17th "	30th "	1st February	22nd "
30th "	21st "	4th December	5th "	26th "
4th October	25th "	8th "	9th "	2nd March
8th "	29th "	12th "	13th "	6th "
12th "	2nd November	16th "	17th "	10th "
16th "	6th "	20th "	21st "	14th "
20th "	10th "	24th "	25th "	18th "
24th "	14th "	28th "	1st March	22nd "
28th "	18th "	1st January	5th "	26th "
1st November	22nd "	5th "	9th "	30th "
5th "	26th "	9th "	13th "	3rd April
9th "	30th "	13th "	17th "	7th "
13th "	4th December	17th "	21st "	11th "
17th "	8th "	21st "	25th "	15th "
21st "	12th "	25th "	29th "	19th "
25th "	16th "	29th "	2nd April	23rd "
29th "	20th "	2nd February	6th "	27th "
3rd December	24th "	6th "	10th "	1st May
7th "	28th "	10th "	14th "	5th "
11th "	1st January	14th "	18th "	9th "
15th "	5th "	18th "	22nd "	13th "
19th "	9th "	22nd "	26th "	17th "
23rd "	13th "	26th "	30th "	21st "
27th "	17th "	2nd March	4th May	25th "
31st "	21st "	6th "	8th "	29th "

Appendix 4. Acknowledgements & Useful Contacts

In compiling this book the author is indebted to numerous people and particularly to the following:

Mrs Alison Lyall who had the unenviable task of proof reading the manuscript.

Mrs Emma Watts for her computer skills which enabled the manuscript to be transformed into a professional publisher-ready book.

Mr Marc Henrie for allowing the use of photographs.

Anatoli Krassavine & Valentina Koulagina (photocat) for allowing the use of photographs.

Mr Alan Robinson for allowing the use of photographs.

All the above devoted their time and expertise gratis.

Publications referred to include:
Somali Cat Club literature, particularly the recommended breeding policy for cats.

The Somali Enigma by M. Frayne PhD.

FAB literature.

Useful Contacts

The Somali Cat Club - www.somalicatclub.com

The Governing Council of the Cat Fancy, 5 Kings Castle Business Park, The Drove, Bridgwater, Somerset. TA6 4AG - www.gccfcats.org

International Cat Care (formerly The Feline Advisory Bureau, aka FAB) - www.icatcare.org